Reaching
New Heights

Other books in the Zonderkidz Biography Series:

Reaching New Heights

the
Kelly Clark
Story

Natalie Davis Miller

ZONDERVAN.com/
AUTHORTRACKER
follow your favorite authors

ZONDERKIDZ

Reaching New Heights
Copyright © 2012 by Natalie Davis Miller

This title is also available as a Zondervan ebook.

Visit www.zondervan.com/ebooks

Requests for information should be addressed to:

Zonderkidz, 5300 Patterson Ave SE, Grand Rapids, Michigan 49530

Library of Congress Cataloging-in-Publication Data

Miller, Natalie Davis.
      Reaching new heights : the Kelly Clark story / by Natalie Davis Miller.
         p. cm.
      Includes bibliographical references and index.
      ISBN 978-0-310-72542-8 (alk. paper)
       1. Clark, Kelly, 1983– 2. Snowboarders—United States—Biography.
   3. Snowboarding—United States—Juvenile literature. 4. Christian
athletes—United States—Biography—Juvenile literature. I. Title.
GV857.S57M57 2012
796.939092--dc23
   [B]   2012029299

Cover design: Kris Nelson
Interior composition: Greg Johnson/TextbookPerfect

Printed in the United States of America

12 13 14 15 16 17 18 /DCI/ 22 21 20 19 18 17 16 15 14 13 12 11 10 9 8 7 6 5 4 3 2 1

*For my wonderful husband, Greg,
and our precious girls, Taylor and Sydney.
Thank you for believing in me.
I love you.*

A Message from Kelly Clark

Snowboarding is a unique sport—it allows you to challenge yourself and reach new heights. Most importantly for me, it was the place where I found God. When I started snowboarding, I didn't know who God was. I didn't even know how to approach faith and religion. But now that God is in my life, others see the happiness, goodness, and fullness that come from knowing Jesus.

I hope you enjoy this book. And if you take anything away from it, let it be the knowledge that you can be an awesome person who lives powerfully instead of being persuaded by the people and circumstances around you. Be who you are called to be and always reach for new heights.

—*Kelly Clark*

Table of Contents

Chapter 1

A Big Blast of Powder

U.S. Olympic snowboarder Kelly Clark watched as the monstrous avalanche moved down the hill, gaining speed and force. Inside that powdery mass of uncontrollable snow was her friend and fellow snowboarder. Kelly unstrapped her boots from her snowboard and ran—shouting and praying—to the area where her friend would most likely be deposited. Kelly had gone down the mountain first, and she was the first person on the scene. Thoughts raced through her brain: *Dig her out, resuscitate her—bring her back from the dead, if necessary.* Kelly had to move quickly. When the snow swallows a body whole, only a few seconds separate life from death.

Kelly thought of the science behind an avalanche. The melting, refreezing, and new fallen snow create layers that are unable to bond together, so they move and slide over each other. Snow on the side of a mountain can become an avalanche from the addition of one simple factor: a person moving down the snow.

"You can prepare as much as you can, you can be as smart as you can, and you can be educated and take as many safety courses as possible; but when it comes to backcountry snowboarding, sometimes that isn't enough," said Kelly. "You are out there in nature, and you can't control everything."

Kelly and her friend were backcountry snowboarding in New Zealand. Together with their guide, they'd flown to the location by helicopter and been dropped off on the mountaintop. Kelly was the first one down, navigating trees, rocks, crevasses, and cliffs—all the rugged features you'd expect to find on a snow-covered mountain.

Before their run, they'd flown over the area by helicopter and checked the zone from the air. They took photos, looked at the lines they wanted to run, and carefully planned where they wanted to go. They planned well; and in doing so, they also planned for the possibility of things going badly.

"You think about everything, and this area looked to be the safest of the day," said Kelly. While she admits she's done some sketchy stuff in the past with crevasses and ice cliffs where bad things definitely could have happened, the area they chose that day seemed pretty mellow.

Kelly rode her line to the bottom and waited for her friend to do her run. "I'm watching her, and basically the unimaginable happens. Something goes wrong at the very top, which is the worst thing because you have nowhere to go but down," said Kelly. "She had a few cliffs to get over that—if you're not on your feet, they're very scary."

The event happening right before her eyes looked like something you'd see on a TV show, and Kelly felt like one of the actors. A bellowing cloud of snow moved down the mountain, and the whole time Kelly watched for her friend to see exactly where she landed and, ultimately, where to start digging. But as Kelly watched, her friend simply disappeared.

Kelly unstrapped her boots and ran. "I just started running. And all of a sudden, as the snow is settling at the bottom, and I'm [still] running, the thing just spits her out. She gets spit out at the bottom of this huge avalanche, and she is completely fine."

Watching her friend travel down the mountainside in an avalanche was by far the scariest thing Kelly Clark had ever experienced while snowboarding. Yet, even in those seconds while it was occurring, Kelly knew she could call on Jesus. "I'm glad no one was around me because I just started yelling and praying as soon as it happened. They would have thought I was nuts. I'm watching it, and without even realizing it, I'm praying and running at the same time."

People may think she's a crazy snowboarder, and Kelly admits to being a "calculated risk taker." Yet Kelly explained, "I do it at my own level and in my own comfort zone. It's a fine line to walk."

Kelly Clark is a two-time Olympic medalist, winning a gold medal for the women's halfpipe in the 2002

Winter Olympics in Salt Lake City, Utah, and a bronze medal for the same event at the 2010 Olympic Games in Vancouver. In 2006, she missed the podium by just one spot, coming in fourth in the women's halfpipe at the Winter Olympics in Turin, Italy.

As the winningest female snowboarder, Kelly recently laid down a streak of sixteen wins going back to 2011. Her winning streak ended when she came in second at the Burton U.S. Open in March 2012. The competition was held in her home state of Vermont, where she has a huge fan base. If she was going to break a streak, home was as good a place as any, according to Kelly. At least in Vermont she would be loved, win or lose.

But more important than all of the medals she's earned — and there have been many — Kelly Clark counts herself a Christian. Just like it happened with snowboarding, she didn't start out that way — but it's where she finds herself today. And she's happy to be there.

Kelly Clark Fast Facts

- Favorite Color: Blue
- Favorite Food: Steak
- Favorite Sport (other than snowboarding): Surfing. "Once you get comfortable in the ocean, figure out how the waves work, it's pretty straightforward. Once I'm standing up, it's very similar [to snowboarding]." If you watch Kelly as she enters the pipe, she has a bent arm movement — elbow up and driving down — that is very similar to what you see surfers do.
- Favorite Movie: *Rudy*. "I really like inspirational sports films."
- Favorite Book: *The Magician's Nephew* by C. S. Lewis. Also, *The Shack* by William Paul Young
- Nickname: Clark-O. "It kind of originated in Japan because they put an 'o' on the end of things, and we had a lot of contests and spent a lot of time over there. They would announce 'Kelly Clark-O.' So all of my friends liked the name, and it kind of stuck."
- Biggest Risk: Snowboarding. "I pursued something that was very new and not widely accepted. It was a mystery as to what the future would be. I put aside years of ski racing and pursued something that I had no guarantee that anything profitable would come of it."

Chapter 2

A Snowboarder Is Born

Kelly Lauren Clark was born on July 26, 1983, in Newport, Rhode Island. She has a brother, Tim, who is five years older. As a baby Kelly was quiet. She rarely cried and always "went with the flow," said her father, Terry Clark. Her first word was *Im*, for her brother Tim. She took her first steps at nine months. And then she learned how to ski.

Kelly hit the slopes for the first time at the age of two, and she took to skiing with ease. "Outside activities in Vermont are very important," said her dad, an avid skier. "Skiing is my life in sports."

The fast, unknown craze of snowboarding hit Kelly when she was seven years old and tried snowboarding for the first time in Stowe, Vermont. On that day Kelly's father realized she had a gift of balance. He recognized very early on that Kelly was special when it came to

Clark Family

Kelly shows a winning smile in her preschool photo. The family lived in Rhode Island at that time.

snowboarding—the sport that she would one day come to rule.

Kelly and her family lived in Rhode Island until she was seven. "It was a small city—you could ride your bike down to the corner store and walk downtown," said Kelly. Eventually, the family moved to the village of West Dover in Dover, Vermont, where they owned TC's Family Restaurant.

Now they spent their summers living on a boat anchored off Block Island, near Newport, Rhode Island, and their winter months at Mount Snow in West Dover. "We constantly did weekend trips throughout the whole winter between Rhode Island and Vermont. And then eventually, when I started going to school, we ended up in Vermont full time," said Kelly.

The family spent time apart during the summers while Kelly's dad worked at the restaurant. On the day school got out for summer break—that afternoon—Kelly's mom and the two kids left for Rhode Island, and they stayed there until Labor Day when school started up again.

Fun in the sun was ingrained as a Clark tradition long before Kelly came along. "I think the week my mom had me she was at the beach," said Kelly. "When I was a kid, I pretty much lived in the water. I was at the beach all day, every day, every summer—playing, swimming, snorkeling, diving, and jumping off the dock."

During those summer months, the Clarks lived on a boat—a twenty-five-foot Bayliner. Many of Kelly's childhood friends were from Block Island, and their families were doing the same thing—spending their summers vacationing while living on a boat. Even today when Kelly goes home, the family vacation agenda usually includes spending time together on the ocean.

Kelly enjoyed small-town life in West Dover as well. "In Mount Snow, there were twelve kids in my sixth grade class, so that's a really small town," said Kelly. The town was a tourist attraction, with visitors hitting the slopes along with the locals. "I spent my weekends at the mountain in the base lodge. That's where all of my friends were, and [it's] where I hung out."

Even at this age, Kelly always wanted to hang out with her brother Tim. "I don't think he thought it was that cool to have his little sister tagging along," said Kelly. "I might have been the annoying little sister who wanted to be cool like her older brother." They had plenty of together time, hitting the mountain, hanging out and watching movies, and long car rides with the family to Florida where they did lots of surfing.

For Kelly and Tim, it was the classic big brother-little sister relationship. Tim thought having his little sister tag along was sometimes good and sometimes not so good. "I threw her down the steps in a sleeping bag once, when we were having sleeping-bag races down the stairs," said Tim. "I take credit for why she is so tough now."

Kelly called Tim a protective older brother. "If anything ever happened to me, he would step in," she said. And the guys in her life always knew that Tim was her big brother.

According to Tim, Kelly was the quiet and serious

one—the "golden child." And he was the one who often got in trouble—trouble that sometimes included his sister. Like many big brothers, Tim knew he could have some fun with his little sister—even if it was at her expense. "Sometimes I think he [took] advantage of how young I was," said Kelly. "I remember one time my parents left money on the counter for something, and he convinced me that it was so I could buy candy. I spent, like, forty bucks on candy. Who would sell forty dollars [worth] of candy to a seven-year-old?" said Kelly. "It seemed like a good idea at the time, but I ended up getting in a lot of trouble. It got dramatic when my parents found out what had happened."

Tim owned up to his role as the mastermind of the candy caper, but that doesn't mean he took responsibility for it. "I blamed it on Kelly and then ate the candy," said Tim. "I used to blame a lot on my little sister."

Kelly also blamed herself for what happened. "I was partly mad that he had convinced me, and kind of mad that I had actually been silly enough to believe that."

When Tim was in college, Kelly was in junior high and high school, so they weren't as close during that time. But like their parents, Tim recognized Kelly's talent in snowboarding. He didn't know how far the sport of snowboarding would go. He didn't attend many of Kelly's snowboarding competitions in the beginning—partly due to his being away at college. But things changed when she was featured in the world's biggest competition—the Olympics.

"It was surreal and crazy that she was the best in the

Thirteen-year-old Kelly celebrates her brother Tim's birthday.

world. I wonder if *I* should have switched to *snowboarding*," Tim joked. He's proud of his little sister, and now that they're both adults, the two of them hang out when they can.

Chapter 3

Puppy Love

Terry Clark, Kelly's father, was born in Waterbury, Connecticut, where he grew up with his brother Richard. At the age of eight, Terry learned to ski, a sport that would soon become his passion. He attended boarding school at Cheshire Academy in Connecticut, where he was the co-captain of the varsity swim team. He graduated from Babson College in 1967, and from there he did some traveling. After working a brief stint for his father at the electric company—a job he wasn't really into—he eventually pursued his love of the "pow" (snow) by ski bumming and managing restaurants and hotels in ski towns.

Kelly's mother, Cathy, was born in New York City. She had two siblings: a sister named Liz, and a brother named Steve. During her elementary school years, Cathy's family moved to West Dover, Vermont. After

Clark Family

Kelly takes time out at her family home with family pets Peanut and Sam.

Cathy graduated from high school, she met Terry, who happened to be running a hotel in West Dover at the time. Cathy skied a little bit, but the two actually met through their dogs.

"They both had Golden Retrievers," said Kelly. "My dad put an ad in the paper because he wanted to breed his dog, and he was looking for a stud. My mom had the stud. My mom called my dad, and [how they met] was kind of like *101 Dalmatians*." The two went from puppy love to marriage four years later.

Dogs have remained a passion for the Clark family, so of course Kelly has always loved having pets. Kelly grew up with two Goldens—Sammy kept her company through elementary school, and Peanut was her pet through middle school and high school. She even has a photo of Peanut wearing her Olympic gold medal around her neck.

Terry and Cathy currently have two dogs. "We breed Goldens, so we cycle through each of our dogs," said Kelly. They allow the dogs to have four litters before having them spayed and neutered. And then they keep one pup from the last litter. "We've had Golden Retrievers for as long as I can remember."

Though Kelly's mother never skied as much as her father did, the Clarks are a family of skiers. And at two years old, Kelly was no exception. With a father who's an official "ski bum," his passion affected the whole family. "Pretty much as soon as we could walk, we were on skis," said Kelly. "At two years old, he had us up there on the mountain." Not much later, Kelly was enrolled in a development program—a weekend program of ski development. By the age of five, Kelly was ski racing. "I skied every chance I had when I was at the mountain, anytime I had available."

The transition from skiing to snowboarding wasn't easy for Kelly or her parents. If there was ever a time that she rebelled as a child, choosing snowboarding over skiing was it. "My parents were really into [skiing], and they wanted to see me be a ski racer," said Kelly. But I had ski raced since I was two, since before I had a choice. It wasn't a road I was pushed down, but a road that was kind of put in front of me and that I was traveling down—whether I wanted to or not."

Snowboarding was still a new and relatively untried

sport when Kelly picked it up. "It was a little bit of a bumpy road," said Kelly. "I always say that I started snowboarding before it was cool. A lot of people kind of thought it was a passing fad—that it wouldn't really catch on."

Kelly enjoyed skiing; but at such a young age, she wasn't into the competitive nature of it. "So although I loved skiing and it was fun, I didn't enjoy the competitive side of things. When snowboarding came along, it looked like fun—free and different, and there wasn't the pressure of competition attached to it. Little did I know, but at that time it seemed like an alternative to skiing that was less serious."

Eventually skiing gave way to snowboarding when Kelly was seven years old. Her first snowboard was a black-and-hot-pink Mogul Monster from Kmart. The official switch happened when she was part of a ski-racing program, and it was discovered that she'd been skipping her lessons.

"I would go up for ski racing every morning and practice and train in the afternoon," said Kelly. Except she wasn't training at skiing. "I would just practice and go snowboarding because my snowboard was in my ski locker. It worked really well until my coach called my dad and asked him if I was feeling okay because I wasn't in the ski-racing program they were paying for.

"Looking back, it's really funny. I used to think I was like a genius because I would leave my snowboard boots at home, and I'd actually strap into my snowboard bindings in my little ski boots so I could go snowboarding. That's how much I really liked it.

Kelly at home with her first snowboard, a pink and black Mogul. She was just seven years old.

Clark Family

"And so it was kind of a big blow-up with my parents. It was a really tough thing because my parents, at that point, had invested money into the ski-racing program, and I just didn't want to have anything to do with it. I wanted to do this thing that was just a fad, and no one even knew if it would be a legitimate sport someday."

The freedom of snowboarding was appealing to Kelly. It wasn't so much an issue of skiing not being fun—Kelly had lots of friends who skied and enjoyed it. For her, the issue was the setting and the competitive nature attached to the skiing. Kelly saw ski racing as just one thing—racing against the clock. It wasn't fun for her. It lacked the creativity and individual style that she found in snowboarding.

She also liked the snowboarding community. Kelly describes it as a "lifestyle sport," a sport with a surrounding culture and a lot of room for self-expression. "I haven't seen a sport that is like it anywhere else. There is a genuineness and a camaraderie that exist between the competitors, even at my high level of competition," said Kelly.

The exhilaration of snowboarding brought hours of enjoyment, fun, and freedom for Kelly. It didn't matter to her whether it was going to be popular or profitable. "I thought, 'Well, if nothing else, I love this more than anything. I'll trade it all for it.'"

Kelly views this period as a tough time for her parents. They'd invested in her for one sport but found that she loved another. And the fact that it was a relatively new and untested sport didn't help matters. Even though Terry knew early on that Kelly was gifted at snowboarding, the concept of it being a sport or a career was beyond him. "I told her there was no future in snowboarding—it wouldn't last, and she should get back to skiing." Terry believed, or perhaps hoped, that his daughter would get tired of snowboarding and move on to other things.

Kelly held her ground on snowboarding and eventually her parents caved. "I was like, 'I'm going to keep skipping ski-racing practice if you keep paying for it, so it's not what I want to do.' I think it was difficult; but after that season, I didn't have ski racing and I just

Kelly showing off early skills at seven years old, riding on Mount Snow, Vermont.

snowboarded on the weekends for fun. At that point I never dreamed of competing in snowboarding. I just really loved the sport." Ultimately, her parents wanted her to do what she wanted and what she liked.

Kelly entered not only a *new* sport, but also a sport in which women had yet to make their mark. Without many girls snowboarding or even competing, Kelly found guy friends to snowboard with. She started taking lessons when she was nine.

At the time, Kelly and her parents had no idea snowboarding would become an Olympic sport. And they certainly didn't know their daughter would eventually become the sport's reigning female champion.

Today, Kelly says she hasn't skied in more than ten years. "Everyone [in my family] actually skis, and I'm kind of the black sheep—the snowboarder."

❄ ❄ ❄ ❄ ❄

Snowboarding: The Birth of a New Sport

"It's a real good sport. I hope everybody gets into it because it's pretty safe. It's a lot of fun. There's a lot of speed and you can definitely surf the snow." Jake Burton spoke those words at the National Snowsurfing Championships at Suicide Six Ski Area in Woodstock, Vermont, back in 1982. Who knew that snowboarding, then in its infancy, would take off to be the world recognized Olympic sport and favorite winter pastime that it is? Burton knew then, and the world knows now.

Snurfer. Skiboard. Snowboard. All words to describe that piece of material you stand on while sailing down the side of a mountain, or laying down tricks in fresh powder. It's fair to say that the history of snowboarding began well before the gathering of competitors in Woodstock in '82. *TheHistoryOf.net* takes snowboarding back to the 1920s when plywood or wood from barrels was bound together to make a board. Even those rudimentary boards had horse reins or clothesline to keep the rider's foot on the board. M. J. "Jack" Burchett is credited with making such a device in 1929. According to *Random History and Word Origins for the Curious Mind,* single planks or sleds were developed and patented in the early 1900s. A "skiboggan" with a hinged stabilizing handle made an appearance in the 1920s. But it wasn't until the '60s that the world saw people actively creating and producing boards for the snow.

Reaching New Heights

In 1963, Tom Sims was just 13 years old. Working in a shop class at school, Sims built his own snowboard, which he dubbed the Skiboard. Probably the most well-known inventor of what would become today's snowboard is Sherman Poppen, a chemical gases engineer from Muskegon, Michigan. Inspired by watching his daughter standing on her sled as she went down a hill, Poppen put two skis together and attached a rope for balance. The Snurfer (a combination of the words *snow* and *surfer*) was born. The Snurfer became popular, and Poppen had them mass-produced and sold. Eventually Poppen put together competitions, drawing in one soon-to-be-well-known competitor — Jake Burton.

The evolution of the snowboard continued when Dimitrije Milovich was inspired to make snowboards after making his way down hills on a cafeteria tray while he was in college. In 1972, Milovich started the company "Winterstick" in Utah, selling his boards in eleven countries. A 1974 *Ski Magazine* cover featured a Winterstick, making it the first time a snowboard had been featured there. The board was also mentioned in *Newsweek*, *Playboy*, and *Powder* magazines. Eventually, Winterstick would make an exit from the snowboarding business in 1980.

The '70s saw a proliferation of snowboard makers. Michael Olsen went the same route as Tom Sims, building a snowboard in his high school shop class in 1977. He played around with building snowboards, eventually dropping out of college in 1984 to begin his snowboard company, GNU. Sims was beyond his high school shop class and was also producing snowboards in California in the '70s. Working with Chuck Barfoot, a surfer and skilled carpenter, the two would eventually hook up with Bob Weber from Maryland to make the "Flying Yellow Banana" skiboard. In 1978, they met brothers Jay and Jeff Grell. Jeff invented high-back bindings, giving boarders more control.

While all of these inventions moved the snowboarding business forward, it can be said that Jake Burton probably did more to move the sport and industry of snowboarding further. Working on the East Coast, Burton moved to Vermont in 1977 where he began cranking out snowboards that featured heel straps for attaching both feet to the boards.

The '80s saw snowboarding competition heat up. In 1982, Snurfer Paul Graves organized the National Snow Surfing Championships at Suicide Six Ski Resort in Vermont. In 1983, Jake Burton took over; moved it to Stratton Mountain, Vermont, in 1985; and renamed it the U.S. Open Snowboarding Championship. Tom Sims sponsored the first World Cup of Snowboarding in Soda Springs, California. The first halfpipe was introduced to the world at the World Cup.

Snowboarding was picking up speed, and riders had a choice of styles. The West Coast featured Sims' freestyle halfpipe riding, while the East Coast played host to Burton's downhill racing style. Magazines were now covering the new sports craze. Yet there would remain one stumbling block to progressing the sport even further. There's nothing like having a new sport with nowhere to play it.

Even though there were more boards hitting the market and more serious riders hitting the slopes, resorts decided they just didn't want to play along. The snowboarding culture was young, loud, and rowdy compared to the more civilized skiing population. Some ski resorts actually banned snowboarders. Others said the cost of insurance was an issue. Still others tried to certify their snowboarders. Finally, there were attempts at managing the youth culture, including their language and behavior.

Even though initially the snowboarding culture wasn't welcomed to take to the slopes next to skiers, the ski resorts did recognize one thing about the riders — they brought in business. As the ski industry began taking a downturn, the new sport of snowboarding was revving up. "Tensions grew as resorts opened to snowboarding, which provided a vital, young demographic to revitalize a struggling industry," cites *RandomHistory.com*. "It proved [to be] the right move as hundreds of new snowboarding companies emerged in the late 1970s and into the 1990s."

A whole new world of interest grew up around the snowboarding industry. The first magazine dedicated to snowboarding, originally called *Absolute Radical*, came out in 1985. Later the name was changed to *International Snowboarding Magazine*. Films were made on the sport. The North American Snowboard Association (NASBA) was formed in 1987. This is the same year that *TransWorld Snowboarding Magazine* published its first issue.

And when the ski resorts decided to play along, they realized they would need dedicated areas for their snowboarders. In 1990, Doug Waugh was tasked with making what would be called the Pipe Dragon. Described as a "giant piece of farm machinery," it made smooth halfpipes. "With halfpipes easier to build and maintain, more pipes and terrain parks started popping up across the country, giving snowboarding's freestyle revolution even more momentum."

By 1990, snowboarding had found its place on top of the mountain. The United States of America Snowboard Association (USASA) sponsored the national championships in February of that year, at Snow Valley, California. It happened to occur during a terrible snowstorm, which closed roads and prevented snowboarders from making it to the competition. That is, until the USASA president helped sneak the snowboarders past police barricades so they could compete in the contest.

The year 1990 also saw the formation of the International Snowboard Federation (ISF). Professional skateboarders and wave surfers were taking to the snow in growing numbers. Contests were heating up all around the globe. ESPN's Extreme Games were born in 1995, and one year later the games got a name change to the X Games, making it more translatable for international audiences, as well as more easily branded.

In 1997, the inaugural Winter X Games were hosted at Snow Summit in Big Bear Lake, California, where snowboarding was featured. The games were televised in 198 countries, and more than 38,000 spectators were on hand to take in the live show. All of this primed snowboarding to be presented in the world's biggest athletic platform, and it was one more place the new sport needed to conquer in order to be truly recognized in the world. The Olympics would give this sport and its riders the chance to show the world that they were here to stay.

Chapter 4

School Days

Kelly continued snowboarding for fun, and at age fourteen she started being coached. When she entered the ninth grade, her school year was divided between two schools, with the snowboarding season sandwiched in the middle. Kelly attended a traditional school during the first quarter, spent the second and third quarters at a mountain school, and then returned to her traditional school in the last quarter.

During the off-season, Kelly attended Brattleboro Union High School in Brattleboro, Vermont. During snowboarding season, Kelly was a student at Mount Snow Academy (MSA) in Mount Snow, Vermont. MSA offered a full-time winter program for skiers and snowboarders in grades six through twelve. While at MSA, Kelly split her day between the classroom and the slopes.

"You take your classes and get tutored during the two

middle semesters [at the mountain school]. You keep up with your course curriculum and go back to your [other] school in the spring," explained Kelly. "It's focused around furthering your snowboarding and pursuing your dreams and accomplishing your academics at the same time." At that point in her life, Kelly knew she wanted to compete in snowboarding and pursue it as her career.

Attending the mountain school came with other benefits—tutoring. Kelly had a speech impediment and had taken speech classes until the sixth grade. But then it was discovered that she also had dyslexia.

Kelly's learning problems initially were undetected partly because she attended a small elementary school where she received more attention and assistance. But her middle school classes had more students. "I was having a hard time as I went from a small school to a big school," recalled Kelly, "which was probably magnified since I wasn't getting as much one-on-one attention."

Kelly had been having trouble keeping up with the rest of the class, so she was tested to find out why. "It's never fun being identified as having some sort of learning disability. But at the same time, through figuring that out, all of a sudden ... things made a lot more sense. And with tutoring and extra help, I could keep up. It wasn't that [I'm not] intelligent; it was just the type of learning environment didn't suit my intellect."

The smaller setting of the mountain school was a perfect fit for Kelly's learning style, but the larger classes in her hometown school presented more of a challenge. So her grandfather made a deal with her: He'd help financially support her while she attended the Mount Snow Academy, but she'd have to improve her grades. "Having an opportunity to get tutored and to pursue snowboarding really seemed like it would work," said Kelly.

After having the dyslexia identified and receiving some tutoring, Kelly's grades did improve. "As soon as I got tutored—that was the type of learning that really helped me."

The teachers at Mount Snow put in a great deal of time to work with Kelly and bring her up to speed. "I was able to not just survive school, but I started to excel. And I think it was the one-on-one tutoring that really facilitated that." Excelling for Kelly didn't necessarily mean how she stacked up against the other students. For her it was the feeling of, " 'Oh, I actually understand this, and I'm actually on track with the rest of my class.' That was *excelling* for me."

With her schoolwork under control, Kelly was able to spend more time playing sports. In addition to snowboarding, she played soccer and tennis. Kelly's transition between Brattleboro Union High School and MSA occurred during those two sport seasons. So playing those sports made it easier for Kelly to go back and forth between her two high schools and still have friends.

"It was nice," said Kelly. "I came back and played tennis immediately, and so I was already in a little group [of friends] right when I got home. I made my friendships back very quickly through sports. If I didn't have that, it would have been really hard to transition in and out of school."

Clark Family

Kelly and her brother Tim celebrate at her graduation from
Brattleboro Union High School in Brattleboro, Vermont. Kelly was
seventeen.

Snowboarding defined Kelly as she went between the two schools. It was how people knew her. "I was the snowboarder. And for good or bad, it was just nice to have it to identify with." Kelly missed out on some of the normal intricacies of high school, but she had her budding professional snowboarding career to focus on.

Snowboarding allowed Kelly to make friends who didn't attend either high school. One friend, Damon Redd, has remained close over the years. The two met when they were twelve years old. "There were a bunch of us skiing around Mount Snow; a couple different groups met up. Little did we know we were making multiple friends for life," said Damon. He attended the junior prom with Kelly at her high school, and apparently Kelly had skills beyond the slopes. "We were dancing fools!" recalled Damon.

Damon spent time with Kelly doing the things teenagers do. "We used to just hang out, play games — raid her parents' restaurant for food. We became workout buddies for a while, going to the Grand Summit Hotel four to five days a week. She was doing training and conditioning for snowboarding. I just worked out to look good."

Chapter 5

A Family Affair

Kelly's first job was at the family restaurant doing odd jobs like using the "pickle bucket" to pick up trash in the parking lot. The pickle buckets were the large five-gallon buckets that pickles came in. A supply of buckets was kept on hand and used for everything, including collecting the trash that appeared in the parking lot after the snow melted.

In Vermont, kids can start working officially at age fourteen. Once Kelly reached that golden age, she started busing and waiting tables at her parents' restaurant, TC's Family Restaurant in West Dover, Vermont.

Kelly describes her parents as hardworking, fun-loving people. They've owned their restaurant for thirty-five years now. "They're both pretty easy-going—they're informal. They've owned a restaurant for as long as I can remember. My dad's more business-minded, maybe a little more serious than my mom. They are both doers—they get stuff done," said Kelly. "They always have projects. They're always doing things." Even now when Kelly goes home for a visit, she knows it's highly likely that she will be given a list of projects that her parents want her to tackle.

Kelly remembers her parents working twelve-hour or longer days during the Christmas season, a busy time for their tourist town. "You could tell how late and how tired they were by how quickly our Christmas presents were wrapped," recalled Kelly, speaking fondly of the haphazardly wrapped gifts. "They were wrapping our presents and putting them out after work at twelve in the morning."

The Clarks' work ethic clearly rubbed off on Kelly, and she wasn't a stranger to hard work. "As soon as I was old enough, I joined them [at the restaurant] as well. From when I was fourteen, I worked the same as they did, and it was actually kind of nice around Christmas and the holidays. Everybody could go away and be with their families because our family was working together."

The family that works together plays together. If it's possible to making dishwashing fun, Kelly's dad found a way. "My dad—he always had a thing—'diving for pearls in the pot sink,' which was a nice way of saying *dishwashing*," explained Kelly. When Kelly was younger, she'd help her brother who started working in the kitchen before she did. "My dad would throw quarters and stuff in the sink every once in a while for us to find, and we'd think it was pretty awesome finding extra money."

Clark Family

TC's Family Restaurant in West Dover, Vermont, was both work and home for the Clarks, who also lived above the restaurant. Celebrity status forced Kelly to sneak in and out of her home.

The family fun was multiplied when Kelly's high school friends also worked at the restaurant. "We'd all work in the same location, and even though on Friday and Saturday nights we wouldn't always get to do fun stuff, we'd all be together at least."

Nothing much out of the ordinary happened while Kelly worked at the restaurant, with the exception of the occasional grease trap backup. This made for great drama with water all over the kitchen floor. The purpose of a grease trap is to collect the fat, oil, and grease (FOG) waste, along with other larger food particles, to keep the sewer lines clean. "That was usually just pretty gross," recalled Kelly.

Kelly worked at the restaurant until she was about eighteen. By that time she'd started traveling full time with her snowboarding, and she'd become a bit of a celebrity, often getting stopped by her fans. "I couldn't walk around and not be talked to," said Kelly. Sometimes she had to go the Hollywood superstar route of wearing hoodies and hats, using the back stairs, and being incognito just to be able to function on a day-to-day basis.

"For a while it became pretty difficult for me to even come and go from the house without being stopped and having to talk to people. It's great that people can be inspired, but it doesn't always conform to a day-to-day schedule." But Kelly has never been one to ditch her fans, and whenever someone approached her, she took time to sign autographs.

Today, the family's restaurant houses all of the hardware that Kelly has accumulated from her many competitions—trophies, her Olympic uniform and medals, including her gold medal. "You look at winning an Olympic medal, and you start to think, 'Well, where should I keep it?' It's certainly valuable and you want people to be able to see it, but it's not something you necessarily want to carry around with you every day. So we thought putting it on display at the restaurant might be a good place for it."

A local blacksmith and sign maker worked together to make a display case that is virtually indestructible and impenetrable. "I've been accumulating a lot of trophies and things that are pretty interesting. It's nice to have a place to put them so people can enjoy them," said Kelly.

Working in her parents' restaurant was time well spent. She learned a great deal about life, hard work, and being responsible. "I'm very organized. I'm very responsible," said Kelly of the person she is today. "As I grew up, I had a lot of life experience and responsibility at a young age. I'm really thankful [for] having grown up working in my parents' restaurant and getting summer jobs because it gave me a good perspective and good work ethic."

Today, Kelly sees kids coming into the snowboarding industry who've never had a real job. She sees they don't have a sense of work ethic or what the real world is all about. But Kelly entered into the fast-paced world of professional snowboarding with a good foundation. "My parents brought me up with good values, having learned them firsthand. And I am definitely the person I am today, thanks to them."

Chapter 6

The Road to Success Starts Here

If you're looking for the beginning of Kelly's stellar career, then X marks the spot. The Winter X Games, first begun in 1997, was still in its infancy when it came to Kelly's home mountain in Mount Snow, Vermont, back in 2000. You have to qualify or be an established athlete to be invited to compete in the games. Kelly, at age fifteen, was well on her way to being the rock-star rider she is today, and the X Games organizers could see this. When you add the possibility that they were looking for a good story angle—bringing in the local girl to ride with the big stars—who wouldn't be up for seeing a young gun go up against the best?

An invitation to compete was extended to Kelly in a roundabout way: The organizers first contacted Kelly's school, her coaches, her parents, and then the invitation finally made its way to her. "I was the youngest competitor

[back] then, at least for the women. I think that was appealing to them, so they let me into the contest. That was my big break."

When Kelly first met the man who would become her agent, he asked her what she wanted to do. She told him her goal at that time: to go to the next Olympics—and win. He said, "Alright. We want to get behind you, and we want to help you do that."

Competing in the X Games was a dream for the wild-card snowboarder. The town was excited as well—throwing all of their support behind Kelly. Although she didn't podium, she got fourth place in slopestyle, which was extremely impressive considering the fact that she technically didn't qualify to enter the games in the first place.

Kelly had previously podiumed in the halfpipe competition at the Copper Mountain Grand Prix in Breckenridge, Colorado, getting second place between two of the biggest stars in the sport at that time. Shannon Dunn took first, and Aurelie Sayres came in third. This competition also occurred in 2000, a year that would prove to be very big in the making and shaping of the young snowboarder.

Before 2000, Kelly was already being recognized for her snowboarding skills. In January of 1999, Kelly was featured in *TransWorld Snowboarding* magazine, photographed riding a rail for a grom (young snowboarder) feature. Later that same month, she won the ISF Continental Cup Boardercross and took first at the X-Nix U.S. Junior Championships in Okemo, Vermont.

She also took the number two spot at the podium in the halfpipe at the same event.

Back home at Mount Snow, Kelly won the Swatch Palmer Boardercross, and she did it again at Sugarbush, Vermont, the very next day. A week later she took second in the halfpipe in the Green Mountain Series.

Kelly's first big win of 2000 was the U.S. Grand Prix in Breckenridge, Colorado. And then came the X Games on Mount Snow. Kelly competed in boardercross, the halfpipe, and slopestyle at her first Winter X Games. Her best result was a fourth in the slopestyle; and interestingly enough, her worst performance came in the halfpipe, which is actually her area of specialty.

The year 2000 saw many more wins for Kelly. She was making a name for herself in the halfpipe, picking up a first at the FIS Halfpipe Junior World Championships in Berchtesgaden, Germany. She podiumed again at the Goodwill Games in Lake Placid, New York, getting second in the halfpipe, and third in boardercross. In March, she won the USASA Boardercross Championship in Okemo, Vermont.

By now, the X Games organizers weren't the only ones recognizing Kelly's mad skills on the slopes, rails, and in the pipe. Kelly's performance captured the attention of the company that would soon become her sponsor—Burton Snowboards. She had previously been sponsored by a company named Flight, and then another one named Elan, which both fizzled out. A local pro worked to get Kelly her early sponsorship, and she was picked up by Burton. The sponsorship supports Kelly in her training, traveling, and competitions. Burton, known for its snowboards, remains Kelly's sponsor today.

"You dream about being sponsored, and you know how expensive the sport of snowboarding is and winter sports in general," said Kelly. "You would get a pair of boots, and you would make them last as long as you could. So the whole idea of getting free product was just the most amazing concept you could think of—not just for me, but [for] my parents too. Knowing they didn't have to purchase new equipment for me was a huge relief."

Kelly closed out 2000 with a third place at the U.S. Grand Prix Halfpipe in Okemo, Vermont. And she picked up another title—she became a member of the U.S. Snowboard team. She was just sixteen years old.

"When I got on the U.S. Snowboarding team, that was another big moment in my career." Gretchen Bleiler, who was eighteen at the time, also joined the team. "We locked the keys in the car the first ten minutes we were with the team. We took the heat together, and we've been friends ever since."

Kelly competed in all three X Games events in 2001. She came in first at the Sprint U.S. Snowboarding Grand Prix Halfpipe at Mammoth Mountain, California; she got third in the FIS Halfpipe in Sapporo, Japan; she won the ISF Canadian Masters Halfpipe in Stoneham, Quebec; and she won the X-Nix U.S. Grand Prix Halfpipe and Boardercross in Sunday River, Maine, finishing her season third overall. She also snagged an IPO (Influential People Of) spotlight in *Snowboarder* magazine. In April of 2001, Kelly won the Vans Triple Crown Halfpipe at Sierra-at-Tahoe, California; and she came in second at the Sims World Championship Halfpipe in Whistler, British Columbia.

Kelly graduated from high school in 2001, and with graduation came some major decisions. Snowboarding was still relatively new having had its first appearance in the Winter Olympics in 1998—the same year Kelly decided she wanted to pursue snowboarding as a career. Kelly believed she could make it in snowboarding. She saw that it was becoming more established. Yet she had to convince her parents that her decision was the right one.

College was very important to the Clarks. Kelly wanted to compete professionally, but she wanted her parents' blessing. She relied on her parents for advice, and she respected what they had to say. She didn't want to make a quick decision and possibly throw away her future. "I had one year to prove to my parents that I could make it as a professional snowboarder," said Kelly. The next few months sealed the deal. "I won the Winter X Games, the Olympics, and the U.S. Open all in one season. These are the contests you hope to win once during your career. I won them all when I was one year out of high school."

In January 2002, Kelly won the U.S. Grand Prix Halfpipe in both Mount Bachelor, Oregon, and Breckenridge, Colorado, after which she became an official member of the 2002 U.S. Olympic Halfpipe Team. She also won the Winter X Games Halfpipe in Aspen,

Clark Family

Kelly at age seven with her father, Terry, on Mount Snow. Terry realized early on that Kelly had a gift of balance on the snowboard.

Colorado. The Winter X Games would be the beginning of what would cement her future as a premier snowboarder. Kelly podiumed again and again, taking gold in the U.S. Winter Olympics and pulling down first-place finishes in the U.S. Open Quarterpipe and Halfpipe in Stratton Mountain, Vermont. She finished out 2002 by placing second in the U.S. Grand Prix overall season-end rankings, winning a Women of the Year award from *Glamour* magazine, and being named the Best Action Sports Athlete at the ESPY Awards (Excellence in Sports Performance Yearly). She also finished third in the FIS World Cup in Valle Nevado, Chile, and won the U.S. Grand Prix Halfpipe in Breckenridge, Colorado.

When Kelly took the gold at the 2002 Winter Olympics in Salt Lake City, one of the first things she said to her father was, " 'Does this mean I don't have to go to college?' He was like, 'Yeah, yeah, you're fine.' "

Kelly opted out of college and does not regret it. "I'm not sure I would have applied myself to a college setting," she said. Not going to college was the right thing for Kelly, but she didn't make that decision lightly. And she knows it's definitely not the right choice for everyone. "As a kid it's really easy to think you know everything and [that] what you want to do is right. But the more I've grown up and the more life I've had an opportunity to experience, the more I realize I don't know everything." Kelly laughed about that because she knows it's true. "Pursue relationships with people whose opinions you value," she advised, "because you're not going to be right all [of] the time. I'm really glad [my parents] helped me make those decisions because they did know more than [I did]."

By remaining teachable and allowing people she trusted to have influence in her life, Kelly was able to make better decisions. "When it comes to pursuing your dream, you're not doing it in a way that is foolish. You're doing it in a way that's smart."

Chapter 7

The Mountaintop – The 2002 Winter Olympics

When Kelly reached her first Olympics, she was just eighteen years old. While she'd met many of the world's greatest athletes on the snow, she hadn't yet met God. But that was about to change.

Kelly had been winning big competitions leading up to the Olympics. She was confident, she'd won her qualifiers, and she was "seeded" (ranked) first for the finals, which allowed her to drop in at the last position. In snowboarding, being the last person to go is advantageous because you can watch your opponents' performances and know exactly what you need to do to win. In some instances, you've already won if your competitors' scores aren't better than your previous one.

After Kelly's first run, she was in second place with

just one run left, and she would be the last to go. Kelly will never forget seeing 17,000 screaming people sitting in a stadium built around a halfpipe. She was competing on the largest scale and on the biggest stage ever. And she was competing in her home country. She had just one run left, one moment.

"I remember that day. I actually had to turn up my music louder than normal because every time I would go across the flat bottom, it would get quiet; and then every time I'd hit the wall to do a trick, the noise of the crowd would roar over my headphones," recalled Kelly.

Snowboarders can wear headphones during competition because there is a lot going on around them — announcers, loud music playing, spectators — many distractions. Kelly was in the habit of listening to music whenever she rode. Generally, she'd wear an earbud in just one ear for safety while she was training. But in a contest, she'd have both earbuds in place. "Essentially what I'm doing is creating an environment instead of being influenced by the environment around me," said Kelly.

But the volume of this crowd wasn't typical when you compared it to the halfpipe competitions Kelly had been in previously. She focused and made the decision to do the best run possible. She knew she could walk away with an Olympic silver medal. But second place wasn't what she'd gone to Salt Lake City to get. "I had one opportunity, and I did the run of my life. The most technical, progressive run that anyone had seen until that point."

Kelly (center) sports her Olympic Gold Medal from the 2002 Winter Olympics in Salt Lake City, Utah. She shares the podium with Dorian Vidal (left) and Fabian Rutler (right).

Kelly looked at her coach at the bottom of the pipe and shrugged her shoulders as if to say, "Really?" because she knew she'd put down the run she needed to win. "So I got to sit there with one of my friends and wait for the judges' scores. I got a 47.9 out of 50 points, and it was the best score out there. I won the Olympics in my home country." Kelly's run included a McTwist and a 720. That, along with her amplitude, put her ahead of France's Doriane Vidal and Fabienne Reuteler of Switzerland. "I learned how to go big, to make the airs.

It made sense to me that once you have your amplitude down, when you try the tricks, they're a lot easier because you've got more time to do them," said Kelly.

Kelly's win for the United States, in a sport still new to the Olympics, helped lay the groundwork for snowboarding to be more accepted at ski resorts around the country. In the same *Sports Illustrated* article, Kelly addressed the culture of boarders who'd come off as vastly different from the more civilized skiers who'd ruled the slopes for years. "Snowboarders have their reputations. But my doing this, especially in the U.S., says a lot. Maybe it will shine a light on snowboarding, and people will look at it in a different way."

In the years between the 2002 and 2006 Olympics, Kelly continued to take snowboarding to a new level. During that time period, she took her place on the podium nearly two dozen times in contests around the world. She also found something else she'd been looking for, and it wasn't at the podium — it was at the bottom of the pipe. Kelly had been looking for God, and she didn't even know it. But God knew, and he found her where her passion and desire lived — in the halfpipe.

Kelly's family didn't practice any type of faith while she was growing up. She never went to church on a regular basis until she started going to Lighthouse, the church she attends now in California. Kelly remembers attending church with her grandmother and the occasional sunrise service on the mountain on Easter Sunday before skiing. But there was nothing formal and regular about attending church for Kelly and her family. "I think when I was real little, my parents would say, 'Say your prayers before you to go sleep,' but I barely remember it."

Living life without faith, not knowing God, and not having a relationship with Jesus can be like walking across a circus high wire—but without a net to catch you if you fall. There is a sense of knowing that something is missing; and for many people like Kelly, there's a longing to find it.

Kelly had experienced great success in snowboarding at a very early age. Kelly won many competitions, including Olympic gold in the 2002 Olympics. "By the time I was eighteen, I had accomplished everything that was in my heart to do. A lot of people spend a lifetime pursuing dreams, and I found myself successful by the time I'd graduated from high school." She began to think that being successful equaled happiness. While Kelly was thankful for her success, she found that she wasn't truly happy or fulfilled.

Kelly was looking for something she couldn't find in snowboarding. "In hindsight, I would say most people are looking for love and for acceptance, and I could find that on a day-to-day basis with my snowboarding. I'd go to a contest, and people would applaud, and people would cheer me on and love me for a brief moment ... until I went to the next weekend and the next contest. I was going from contest to contest looking for love, essentially, and even at the highest of heights in athletic achievement, you don't find that."

Kelly didn't know what she was looking for; she just knew she wasn't happy. "I had done everything I could to be successful, and at that point I was exhausted." She felt like there was nothing else she could do to make herself happy. Therefore, she thought life must not be very good. "It is a unique perspective to arrive at that conclusion though all [of] this success, but that was just kind of where I was at," she said.

The year was 2004, and Kelly was just two years out from her '02 Olympic experience. She was at the top of her career—a position anyone would envy—but for her, there was nowhere else to go but down. Competition and winning was something Kelly could maintain, but the pressure was unbelievable. The constant striving for success and acceptance left her feeling like she was inside a giant pressure cooker. "All of a sudden I wasn't just winning to win. I was winning to be happy, and it's not a very fun place to operate out of, and [it's] not very effective as an athlete either. It's difficult to deal with that sort of pressure."

Chapter 8

Finding Faith at the Bottom of the Hill

Kelly journaled her feelings during this time, and one thing she wrote was, "If this is what life is about, I'm not interested." She found herself not caring if she woke up the next day, and she didn't think anyone else would care either. Yet she continued to compete, just going through the motions. "From the outside, I was living the dream that every kid dreams. You're a professional athlete, you have an Olympic gold medal, you're the best at what you do. But on the inside, I was just dying because it was all so hollow for me."

Kelly was at a snowboarding competition in Park City, Utah—the place where she had received her gold medal, the place that put her on top of the world of snowboarding. During the competition, she qualified for the finals. It was business as usual for her. But something changed at the end of her run. She had to come down the mountain to hear what God wanted her to hear.

"I was standing at the bottom, and a girl had come down who had failed to make it to [the] finals. She had crashed twice, and she was crying. I just happened to overhear her conversation with her friend. Her friend was trying to get her to laugh and said, 'Hey, it's all right. God still loves you.'" Even though Kelly had heard that statement before, it stirred something in her that she couldn't pretend wasn't there.

"It hit something in me, something started in my heart that I just couldn't ignore. I didn't know much about God. I didn't know about Jesus. I didn't know anything. I hadn't been to church. I didn't have a grid for anything."

She began to ponder what she had heard. *If God loves them, maybe God would love me.* "For the first time in my life, I thought, 'Well, maybe that's what I've been looking for this whole time.'"

Kelly couldn't let the moment pass. She had to find out more about God. She eventually ended up back at her hotel room where she looked for a Bible. She found the King James Version, but she was like a foreigner in a new land—a foreigner who didn't know the language. Kelly didn't know where to start in the Bible. Again, like a foreigner in a strange land, she would need a guide.

So she found the young lady she'd overheard at the bottom of the hill. Kelly knocked on the door of her hotel room and introduced herself. "I said, 'Hey, my name's

Kelly, and I think you might be a Christian. And I think you need to tell me about God.'"

Like anyone would be, the young lady on the other side of the door was surprised to find herself standing face to face with this high-profile snowboarder who was standing in the hallway and asking her about God. But like any Christian who's called upon to share the Word, she answered the call.

The young woman invited Kelly into her hotel room, and the two began talking. Kelly's newly appointed guide for her spiritual journey told her about God and answered her basic questions—the only questions Kelly knew enough to ask. It was okay not to know where to start—the important thing was that she had started. "I guess at that point I had never had a real experience with God or Christians or church or anything along those lines. For me, it was all new. The only things I thought I knew were stereotypes of ideas."

Kelly had thought being a Christian was about being good all of the time, following rules, and going to church. Her new friend told her it wasn't about being religious. It was about having a relationship with God—which is what we are all created for—and knowing God loves us. "That was a big eye-opener for me because I had never heard that before."

This was great to hear, but it also began stirring things up inside of Kelly. "At the same time, I was kind of nervous because I had never thought about God a day in my life. I had never wondered why we are here, I had never [asked] myself those sorts of questions, and so

I was trying to work out why I cared about this for the first time in my life."

Because it was so new, Kelly approached her newfound faith with caution. Initially, she told herself she wasn't about to just jump into something without weighing it out first. She looked at her sport of snowboarding—a lifestyle sport—and her image as an athlete and professional. She considered what others might think about her finding God. "I was worried about what my sponsors would say. I was worried about what my friends would think, and I was worried about what my family would say if I were to all of a sudden say, 'Hey guys, I've met God and this is the path I want to choose.'" Kelly knew her next steps were important—a "big deal," as she described them.

Kelly spent the next five months seeking God. She surrounded herself with people who could answer her questions. She became friends with the girl she'd met at the bottom of the hill. Dee Tidwell, Kelly's conditioning coach, was also a Christian and influential in her getting to know God better. He gave her a copy of *The Purpose Driven Life* by Rick Warren, a book that Kelly found to be a valuable tool. "I could read stories about people, and I could read about the Word and who God was, and I could see it happening in my life. It became real and it became live and it became my own relationship with him."

Kelly began to think about God every day. She continued to pray and study her newfound faith. At one point she asked herself two simple questions: *Could I wake up another day and not think about God? Could I ever walk away and pretend God doesn't exist?* The answer to both questions was no. As for God's existence, Kelly prayed and read her Bible and, "He would meet me every day, and he was very, very real." She had learned this simple truth: "If you want to know who God is, ask him and he will reveal himself and you will meet him."

By the end of that snowboarding season, the girl who first spoke with Kelly about God and her faith was now asking her if she had accepted Jesus. Kelly was so green to her new faith that at first she didn't understand the question. After studying, and then asking and answering those two questions about God, Kelly made another decision. "I said, 'Okay, Jesus. I welcome you into my life, and I want to live life with you, and I realize I can't do it on my own. I've never been able to, but I know what you've done, Lord, and I'm in.'"

Kelly began attending church with the young lady who first introduced her to Jesus. Her church, the Lighthouse, was in Mammoth, California, where Kelly was now living. Other snowboarders and a few people Kelly knew from town were also members there, and they were surprised to see her. Kelly told them she wasn't sure what she was doing, but she knew there was something to this "God thing."

Looking through the eyes of her friends, Kelly could see where they were coming from. Here she was this high-profile snowboarder who seemingly had everything she could ever need. "It looks like you've got it made. It looks like you're living the dream, but the reality was that there was a lot more that I was looking for that I couldn't find in athletics," said Kelly.

Kelly's faith was new to her family as well. "I think it was quite an adjustment [for them] because when your daughter moves 3,000 miles away to California and comes back and tells you she's found faith in Jesus, it's probably a bit alarming because there isn't much of a reference," explained Kelly. Her family didn't know what it meant to be a Christian or what it looked like to believe in Jesus—other than stereotypes. "I think it definitely was a little bit scary for them," said Kelly. But that eased up as her family saw how much happier and more stable she was, and how much more enjoyable she was to be around. Kelly explained how they became very accepting and supportive of her faith "because my actions speak volumes to what I believe. I'm not saying one thing and doing another. And they can see the fruit of the Spirit as being a good thing in my life."

Kelly's father said he was happy that Kelly had found a way of life that gave her strength and happiness. "Kelly is faith. Nothing else matters," said Terry. "I knew when she told me about what she now wanted in her life that it was the right thing for her at the time. Prior to that day, she was wandering; she was not sure what she was here for. Her faith gives her what she needs in her life. She was put here to snowboard as good as she can, and if that is why she was put here, then it's up to her to do the very best she can, win or lose."

It was clear to them that Kelly had changed and that the change was positive. "My brother sat me down one time and said, 'I don't know whether I understand your relationship with God, but I see *our* relationship is better as a result of your relationship with God.'"

Chapter 9

A New Life in God

Kelly became immersed in her new life and church, and she made new friends. One friend, Karen Phillips, witnessed Kelly's transformation and how she's grown in her Christian faith. Karen is an elder at Lighthouse, which is where she met Kelly. Even though they're from different generations (Karen is married and has children Kelly's age), Karen and Kelly have become very good friends.

Besides their passion for Jesus, the two women also share friends, they both love to travel, and they love the outdoors. They've even gone camping and surfing together. "As a family we have spent holidays with Kelly at our home, and periodically we have traveled with her to events," said Karen. They even attended the Vancouver Olympics. "She is not home here [in Mammoth] for much of the winter. So when she is, our time is like family time."

Karen said Kelly has worked on the church's website, helping Lighthouse connect with international churches. Kelly also travels to other Lighthouse churches and speaks at their meetings. "One of Kelly's strong points is communication and staying connected to people," said Karen.

Even though Kelly is relatively new to her faith, Karen sees how far and how quickly Kelly has grown as a Christian. "I remember thinking the things it took me fifteen years to learn took her a couple of years. She lives what she believes, and when God shows her something new to grow in, she applies herself to study, meditation, and stepping out—taking risks and doing it." Karen said Kelly is a natural at praying for healing in people, praying about the injuries and sicknesses of friends in her industry.

Kelly has experienced firsthand the power of prayer in healing. In 2007, she broke her collarbone. Kelly's doctor told her she didn't displace it, but it would still take six weeks to heal. Needless to say, it was a setback. In addition to the pain, Kelly found she couldn't do simple tasks such as cutting her food, combing her hair, or even getting dressed. She was injured on a Sunday, and on Tuesday she attended a faith conference.

The speaker at the conference asked if anyone there was experiencing pain. Kelly's arm was throbbing. "I stood up, and the people around me prayed for me. And [the speaker] said, 'Do something you couldn't

Kelly at the *NBC Today Show* Studio at Grouse Mountain in North Vancouver, Canada, on February 19, 2010.

Scott Halleran/Getty Images North America

Kelly shows the world how she feels about Christ with her signature snowboard stickers. She waits for her results at the 2012 Winter X Games at Buttermilk Mountain in Aspen, Colorado, on January 27, 2012. Kelly took home the gold in the women's superpipe.

Kelly competes at the U.S. Snowboarding Grand Prix in Killington, Vermont, in March of 2009.

Kelly on the red carpet at the Nokia Theatre in L.A. for the 2011 ESPY Awards.

Kelly Clark of the United States competes in the women's snowboard halfpipe qualification on day seven of the Vancouver 2010 Winter Olympics at Cypress Snowboard & Ski-Cross Stadium on February 18, 2010 in Vancouver, Canada.

Kelly Clark (right) celebrates winning a bronze medal at the flower ceremony of the Snowboard Women's Halfpipe final at the Cypress Snowboard & Ski-Cross Stadium in Vancouver, Canada, at the 2010 Winter Olympics. Hannah Teter (left) of the U.S. brings home the silver, and Torah Bright (center) of Australia is the gold medal winner.

Kelly Clark competes in the ladies halfpipe final during the 2011 Sprint US Snowboarding Grand Prix on March 5, 2011 in Mammoth Lakes, California. Clark won the event.

Kelly gets big air in the ladies halfpipe finals at the March 2011 Sprint Snowboarding Grand Prix in Mammoth Lakes, California.

Kelly Clark rides to first place in the women's halfpipe finals of the Sprint US Snowboard Grand Prix on December 10, 2011 in Copper Mountain, Colorado.

do,' and I was able to lift my arm about eight inches."
Kelly thanked God for the immediate improvement. "I
literally lifted up my arm, and I just started crying and
screaming because my collarbone had gotten miracu-
lously healed. And it wasn't just a little bit healed—it
was 100 percent healed."

Kelly compared the experience to the story of Jesus
healing the blind. Her bone had been knit back together,
and she was able to go mountain biking two days later.
Kelly was left with a reality she had come to know:
"Okay, God, you must be real. You must be really, really real because this is a physical, tangible experience
I've had with you."

Karen has seen how Kelly has grown in her trust in
God, recognizing him as bigger and able to do more than
what she could do herself. "She has an ease with trusting
him, which allows her to be naturally supernatural."

Karen knows the many sides of Kelly—her mellow,
relaxed happy-person side as well as the adventurous
side—and she has the stories to back it up. She's seen
videos from Kelly's camera as it recorded the start of
that avalanche. Kelly has sent Karen photos of herself
bungee jumping from bridges, and once from the top of
a tower in New Zealand—with her snowboard strapped
on. She's gone wakesurfing with friends in Mammoth,
California. And she's gone surfing with the crocs in
Costa Rica. "After the Vancouver Olympics, she was invited to the Vancouver Zoo for a tour—and she kissed a
whale on the lips," said Karen.

Yet in all of her adventures and achievements, Kelly

still finds time for others. After she received her bronze medal, Kelly had the privilege of presenting a coach of the year award to her coach. Karen sees Kelly as a person of great integrity. "She is consistent, authentic, and genuine. She lives from her values and doesn't waiver."

Karen also knows there are some in the snowboarding industry who look to Kelly for advice, wisdom, and personal help. They know Kelly is a good communicator and a good listener. "She is a very safe person to confess [your] innermost thought and fears," said Karen.

Chapter 10

We Fall Down, We Get Up – The 2006 Winter Olympics

Kelly again represented the United States as a snow-boarder in the 2006 Winter Olympics in Turin, Italy. Only this time, in addition to bringing her mad skills to the pipe, Kelly brought God along for the ride. Having her faith in check made dealing with the ultimate outcome of the '06 Olympics easier. In what should have been a stellar, medal-earning performance for Kelly, the worst imaginable thing happened—she crashed.

Heading into the finals, Kelly had won the qualifier and was seeded in the best place. Kelly described her first run as not her most technical run. If anything, it was a safe run, which landed her in third place. "In talking with my coach, I really had to make up my mind and ask myself what I was going to be happy with—would

I be happy with what I attempted? I didn't want to be thinking back on this Olympic experience later in life and saying, 'Wow, I wish I [hadn't] played it safe. I wish I had really given it my all because who knows what the possibility could have been?'"

So there she was in third place. Being the competitor that she was, Kelly wanted to go for it, holding nothing back. "I'm a risk taker, but I'm a calculated risk taker," said Kelly. She told her coach she was attempting her hardest run. "That's what I'm going to be happy with at the end of the day, regardless of what the outcome will be." As Kelly waited her turn, the rider before her scored well and bumped Kelly to fourth place.

"So here I am, there are only two people behind me that are already ahead of me in the standings, and I've got one opportunity left," said Kelly. "I knew I couldn't change my approach based on what was going on around me. That's one of the things I've learned as a person through snowboarding—it essentially comes down to really living from the inside out; making your decisions and making up your mind before you get there."

Kelly knew it would have been easier to play it safe and do an easier run. She could have squeaked into third place. Instead, she chose to do what she'd set out to do—the run of her life. What she got for her efforts was fourth place—what Kelly heartbreakingly refers to as "first loser." Kelly went through a series of tricks—a 12-foot frontside air, two back-to-back 540s, and a 900—but she caught the edge on her last landing, which caused her to just barely set down.

Ricky Bower, the U.S. Snowboarding Halfpipe Coach for the 2014 Winter Olympics, saw Kelly's run as the biggest run ever done by a woman in the finals. More than likely she would have won the contest if she had landed after her trick. "Kelly's run stood out more than the winning run that day because of the sheer size of all her tricks."

Kelly was disappointed—there was no doubt about that. But she also had something with her during this Olympic experience that was absent in 2002—faith. "It was a very difficult decision, but even looking back now, I'm so thankful that I really was living powerfully and living in a way where I didn't let my circumstances dictate the decisions I made.

"I had to reassess things and really be okay with pursuing my dreams again, even at the expense of not achieving them. I couldn't let disappointment and heartache keep me from pursuing my dreams."

Kelly would continue to pursue her dreams—again stepping up to the podium to pick up her hardware. In March of 2007, Kelly snagged a win at the U.S. Open Halfpipe in Stratton Mountain, Vermont. In July, she came in second at the Abominable Snow Jam Halfpipe in Mount Hood, Oregon, taking home the award for Highest Air. August saw her winning the New Zealand Open Quarterpipe and taking second in the halfpipe. In January 2008, she came in third in the Winter X Games Halfpipe in Aspen, Colorado; and in March she won the U.S. Grand Prix Halfpipe in Killington, Vermont. Kelly also picked up the Best Trick and Highest Air accolades in the New Zealand Open Quarterpipe in July 2008.

In 2009, Kelly won the European Open Halfpipe in Laax, Switzerland. Kelly had a textbook year in 2009, and she continued to place in the top three in snowboarding contests around the world. Again, all of her work prepared her to take the world stage in snowboarding—the 2010 Winter Olympics in Vancouver.

Even though Kelly had been posting solid victories, she found it difficult to get ramped up for the 2010 Olympics. She was still coming off the heartbreaking fourth-place finish in the 2006 Olympics. "I think it's really difficult to deal with disappointment and get back up after you've had your heart broken. I think that required a lot more courage than any of my other events."

By the time the 2010 Winter Olympics began, Kelly had an even firmer foundation in her faith and who she was. She listened to Christian music at the top of the pipe, just before her runs. And she wasn't shy about singing along loud enough for those standing close-by (and the event mics) to hear. Kelly became known for singing Christian music at the top of the pipe. "That's where I want to be focused when I'm operating at my best," said Kelly. Some of her favorite artists include Misty Edwards, Anthony Skinner, Ian McIntosh, Kim Walker-Smith, Jake Hamilton, Will Reagan, and United Pursuit.

Kelly let the world know how she felt about her faith when—with the help of a friend who'd started a company called Jesus Stickers—she emblazoned "Jesus" across the bottom of her snowboard. She wanted something that would express what she was passionate about but didn't cross boundaries or offend anyone. The idea of representing Jesus on her snowboard came to her shortly after she was saved. "Snowboards are little places where people can express themselves. A lot of people will take stickers or company logos that they identify with and put them on their boards. As you get into more competitive aspects, you end up putting [on the] stickers of [the] companies you represent," she explained. Kelly also displays the stickers of companies that support her, but the picture wasn't complete until she added her Jesus sticker. "I was thinking the most supportive and biggest part of my life is God." The two stickers you can't miss on her board read "Jesus" and "I cannot hide my love."

Kelly knew it would be difficult to explain to people who she was now, where she was coming from, and what she believed. She wondered if people might make fun of her. She wondered if it would be difficult for her to maintain her beliefs when she wasn't at home and attending church. A song she heard during church one day seemed to supply her with the answer in one of its verses. "I Cannot Hide My Love" by Enter the Worship Circle moved Kelly to prayer. "I felt like God was saying, 'You know your love for me isn't going to be something you have to tell people about. It's going to be something that you're not going to be able to hide.'"

Kelly walked away in peace and with a clear understanding of where she was in her faith. It was then that she approached her friend about making stickers for her board. The stickers are about who Kelly is, not what she's going to tell people. The space on the bottom of her board had become more than a place to express herself. She could look down at her board and see what she valued, what she supported, and who supported her. "And you know now, after the last seven years, it's become a bit standard in my life, and people expect to see it," said Kelly. "It was nice because it wasn't something I had to tell people about. It was something I could not hide."

The 2010 Olympics were kinder to Kelly than the 2006 Games had been. Once again she found herself on the podium. This time she wore a bronze medal and placed behind fellow American Hannah Teter, who won a silver, and Australian snowboarder Torah Bright, who took home the gold. Kelly came in third with a score of 42.2 out of 50 after falling on her first run. Still, Kelly treasured her medal. "This is a very special medal for me because I've worked so hard. Pursuing Olympic dreams is a very hard thing to do after missing the podium by one," said Kelly in a *New York Times* interview. (In 2006, she missed third place by one point.)

With three Olympic appearances and two medals, it was business as usual as Kelly continued her bid for best female snowboarder. Off the snow, she was getting national publicity. She appeared on the *TODAY* show in February 2010, and she was also on the cover of *Pleasure Magazine* in April 2010.

On the snow, Kelly continued to win. And in 2011 she won the Winter X Games Superpipe and stomped a trick that had never been done by a female snowboarder. Kelly owned the frontside 1080.

Chapter 11

Setting the Bar – The 2011 Winter X Games

Even though Kelly is incredibly competitive, her best friends are the women out on the snow with her. "Gretchen Bleiler is probably one of my biggest competitors, and we've been friends for years," said Kelly. She was actually a bridesmaid in Gretchen's wedding. "It's a very unique sport where we are inspired and pushed by one another. When I see my friends snowboarding well, it makes me want to be a better snowboarder." This must be true of her friends too because no one seemed happier to see Kelly land not just *her* first, but also a woman's first-ever frontside 1080 during the 2011 Winter X Games. When Kelly reached the bottom of the hill, her fellow competitors congratulated her by knocking her to the ground in a joyous victory pileup. "That was really a special moment for me because it wasn't just me who was celebrating; it was my friends and my community and my competitors who were rejoicing."

For Kelly, the sport of snowboarding is unique because it's always progressing and changing. "It's constantly growing and developing; and as snowboarders, we get to be part of that, and it makes it really fun because we get to be on the forefront of shaping this sport," said Kelly. "We're continually bridging the gap between what's possible and impossible."

There are certain tricks the men do that the women haven't progressed to, according to Kelly. One was a frontside 1080—basically three full rotations. Kelly had been pursuing the 1080 for a few years, and she'd actually landed it a few times outside of competition. But as she puts it, she hadn't been able to call it her own. But Kelly systematically kept at it. She realized that if she wanted to build up her skills, she would have to build out—she needed a broader foundation. This led her to spend more time on the fundamentals. She worked on the basics—being consistent and being efficient in her edge control. "Having good fundamentals is the best place to build from for bigger tricks," said Kelly.

She also knew she didn't want to be in a competition setting where she *had* to do that trick in order to win. "I wanted to do it because I wanted to—not because I had to." This was Kelly's theme for her season—living intentionally. "Competition or no competition, Olympic year or not, I was going to be out there doing the tricks that I set out to do. Not for anybody else, but for the progression of the sport."

Going into the X Games in 2011, Kelly knew the runs she wanted to make. She knew that in order to free herself up and to live intentionally meant she needed to raise her standards. "I needed to get my easy run—my basic stock tricks that I can do every time—to a point that my easy run would be everyone's hard run."

The X Games proved to be the perfect place to unveil her strategy and her new trick. With three runs, Kelly had the X Games won by her first run. In her second run she crashed. But by her third run, all she had to do was sit back and take a nice, easy victory lap. Still, she wasn't willing to settle for that. She had made up her mind to live intentionally. She'd been practicing and pursuing her 1080. So with the contest already in the bag, Kelly brought the 1080—shocking her competitors, her fans, and the announcers who took a couple of seconds to react.

"Yeah, I think I surprised them. They almost missed it because I had to change up my run because when I was trying it, I had to adapt and change because of the wall, the halfpipe length. So I had to move it up in my run."

Kelly has stomped the 1080 during a few more competitions since then, but she's ready to start working on other things. She compares her accomplishment of the 1080 to the first runner to ever run a four-minute mile— once the door opens, others want to go through. She expects her friends and competitors to come after her with the 1080, but she welcomes the competition.

"We're all competitive, but we all care for one another as well," said Kelly. "It's kind of a unique thing where it's competitive, but it's not cutthroat. It's about striving for excellence. But at the end of the day, I'm usually my biggest competition."

The competition and the camaraderie may go hand in hand because, according to Kelly, the women are doing what they love for a living. Not only is it enjoyable, but they can look to each other for amazement and inspiration as well.

Chapter 12

A Season to Remember

The year 2011 continued to be a good one for Kelly. In addition to winning the Winter X Games and stomping the first-ever women's frontside 1080, Kelly won the O'Neill Evolution Halfpipe Event in Davos, Switzerland; the Burton European Open Pipe in Laax, Switzerland; the Canadian Open in Calgary; as well as the Dew Tour Snow Basin and Overall Dew Cup in Snow Basin, Utah. She won the Mammoth Grand Prix in March, and she won both the Burton U.S. Open in the halfpipe and was the overall leader in the Burton Global U.S. Open (BGOS), a series of competitions staged around the world. That month she also dominated in the Euro X Games. In August, she won the New Zealand Open Halfpipe (for the third year in a row), and then took first at the U.S. Grand Prix at Copper in Copper Mountain, Colorado, in December. That year Kelly was nominated for two ESPY awards. And she continued to be featured in Burton ads.

Her winning season took her into 2012 with a streak of sixteen wins. However, that streak was broken at the Burton U.S. Open in March, where she came in second.

Ten years after winning her first gold, and eight years after finding God at the bottom of the pipe, Kelly continues to strive for excellence in her sport by remaining focused, consistent, and intentional. As a member of the U.S. Snowboarding team, she looks forward to her fourth Olympic appearance in 2014 in Sochi, Russia.

The History of Snowboarding and the Winter Olympics

Snowboarding made its grand entrance at the 1998 Winter Games in Nagano, Japan. The first modern Olympic Games were a project of Pierre de Coubertin in France. Many had tried to bring back the Olympics, but de Coubertin founded the International Olympic Committee (IOC) in 1894 with the aim to organize the first modern Olympics. In 1896, the first modern Olympic Games were held in Athens, Greece. In 1924 the IOC decided to have an International Winter Sports Week in Chamonix, France. Two years later, that event was retroactively named the first Winter Olympic Games.

Until 1992, the Winter Olympics were held during the same year as the Summer Olympics. Now the Winter Olympics are held within two years of the Summer Olympics, but they still maintain a four-year rotation. At that "first" Winter Olympics in 1924, the sports were bobsleigh, curling, ice hockey, figure and speed skating, skiing — cross-country and ski jumping — and the military patrol race.

Little by little, snowboarding gained recognition until it finally appeared in the Olympics. Now fast-forward to 1998 when for the first time, Olympic events included the halfpipe and the giant slalom in men's and women's competitions.

The parallel giant slalom replaced the giant slalom at the 2002 Salt Lake City Olympics. In 2010, the men's and women's boardercross was added. When the Winter Olympics take place in Sochi, Russia, in 2014, spectators will see eight events: men's and women's halfpipe, men's and women's parallel giant slalom, and men's and women's boardercross, along with the addition of snowboard slope-style. Spectators will see all of the action at the Rosa Khutor Extreme Park. The 8,000-seat facility will begin hosting events in 2012, and will continue to feature world-class competition after the 2014 Olympics.

Kelly Clark, who at age eighteen was the youngest member of her 2002 U.S. Olympic Snowboarding team, will make an appearance in her fourth Winter Olympic Games when she competes in the halfpipe event in Sochi, Russia, in 2014. Kelly will be thirty years old then, but the sport of snowboarding will still appeal to the young, and the young at heart.

Chapter 13

Sometimes the Good Die Young

In the midst of a fantastic winning season for Kelly, the entire snowboarding and skiing community found themselves dealing with the tragic death of one of their own. Sarah Burke, a Canadian freestyle skier, died nine days after falling during training on the Eagle Superpipe at the Park City Mountain Resort in Utah. The injury resulted in a tear in her vertebral artery, which led to bleeding on the brain, cardiac arrest, and eventually death.

Burke had won gold at the Winter X Games six times. She'd also lobbied to have superpipe skiing added to the Winter Olympics, and in 2014 it will appear for the first time at the Sochi Olympic Games in Russia.

Prior to the start of the 2012 Winter X Games, Kelly and other athletes joined Sarah's family in a somber tribute to Sarah. After a short video highlighting her life and achievements, the lights were darkened on the superpipe. Quietly, slowly, three rows of athletes moved down the pipe. Each held a lighted tube that gave off a soft candle-like glow. There was no music, no words, no sound except the soft brushing of skis and snowboards against the snow. When the athletes reached Sarah's family at the bottom of the pipe, the crowd erupted into applause, shouts, and whistles. All went quiet again as the athletes delivered hugs and flowers to the family.

The memorializing of Sarah did not end there. Athletes also plastered their gear with stickers that said "Celebrate Sarah" and "Believe in Sarah." Kelly showed her support by wearing her sticker on her helmet. It was proudly displayed as she went on to win her fourth Winter X Games gold medal in the superpipe. Even before Kelly's big win, and before Sarah died, Kelly had rallied other skiers and snowboarders in support of Sarah while she fought for her life in the hospital in Utah. Using Twitter hashtags "believeinsarah" and "prayingforsarahburke," Kelly helped to bring in fans and supporters to a vigil for Sarah in Breckenridge, Colorado.

Kelly remained steadfast and focused on Christ—her faith unshaken—despite the loss of Sarah. "With my approach in snowboarding, I have to hold true to what I am doing and what I believe, regardless of what is going on around me. And this was no exception. I don't understand why bad things happen to good people, and I am okay with that. I will trust in God and hope in him when I don't understand things. But I will not make up some bad theology to support my circumstances that is

Kelly shows her support for Sarah Burke by wearing a "Celebrate Sarah" sticker on her helmet at the 2012 Winter X Games at Buttermilk Mountain in Aspen, Colorado, on January 27, 2012. Kelly won the gold in the women's superpipe.

contrary to who God says he is in the Bible. I will not look at what is going on around me and say for one moment that my circumstances define my belief. I believe he is good all the time and only has good things for us. I am sad and I grieved, but I have peace that only God can give. I will press into him during this time."

Sarah Burke's death reminds us that we are limited, human creatures, while Kelly's faith reminds us that even in the worst of times, there is someone we can turn to. Her perseverance and faith in who she is, and who God is keeps her focused and moving forward to his glory.

Chapter 14

Living Intentionally and Focusing

No matter how strong an athlete's body is or how skilled she is, it won't serve her well if she doesn't have the focus she needs to compete. If there is one thing Kelly has mastered—beyond big air and stomping a perfect 10— it's living intentionally and maintaining focus.

"You can never *lose* focus. You can just be focusing on the wrong thing at the wrong time," said Kelly. "It's almost impossible not to realize what's going on around you. By being in that area, you obtain it. So it's just a matter of what you choose to focus on. It's all up to you."

Kelly compares this type of focus to studies she's read on focusing and visualization. For example, if a person visualizes himself practicing at a sport such as hitting free throws in basketball, or perhaps playing the piano, it has been found to be nearly as beneficial as the actual practice itself. To put herself in that place, Kelly watches videos of herself doing things correctly. "And getting that in my mind really helps me get into the moment, and that's what I'm doing when it's time to focus. You just have to figure out what it takes for you to focus on the task at hand and not be distracted."

For Kelly, it's music and preparation before she gets into the situation. This means knowing what she's going to do if she falls, or if it looks like she won't make it to the finals. By staying focused, she doesn't let a disaster sideline her. "You have to be prepared for the situations and figure out how to refocus," said Kelly.

In addition to music, having people around her to remind her of former victories helps. "Remembering what I've been able to accomplish in the past helps me get through the current distress."

Beyond the slopes, Kelly must maintain who she is when she's in other environments. As a professional athlete, she's often invited to red-carpet events where she's with other superstars—athletes, movie stars, and pop icons. There are a number of things she can be exposed to or influenced by, and not all of it is good.

Kelly handles herself by making decisions and focusing on what is happening *inside herself,* instead of being influenced by what is happening *around* her. In this way, she impacts her surroundings—they don't impact her.

"Essentially what it comes down to is I make my mind up before I get there. I know how I'm going to act, I know what I'm going to say, and I know what I value apart from what's going on around me. And through having that rooted and grounded in my life, I'm able to go from environment to environment and be influential instead of being influenced."

Kelly is a "what you see is what you get" kind of person. She feels she should be the same person on the red carpet at the ESPYS as she is at church, or at the top of the halfpipe at the X Games, or with friends at home. "I try to live a life of consistency—my values are what I live from, and my actions are a representation of that—so I'm able to go from environment to environment."

Prayer is another way Kelly keeps grounded. At some events there are a few competitors who will get together to pray before they compete. Kelly also sends out a prayer email that involves many people praying for her, covering her when she is in the middle of things and not necessarily able to do it all herself.

With so much going on around Kelly—fans, coaches, music blaring over the loud speakers—at the end of the day, the loudest voice she wants to hear is that of the Holy Spirit. "That is my life force and my everything and the most stable thing. So even when I'm in the midst of having a crazy contest or being very successful or scrambling, trying to come back from a fall, that is going to be the biggest thing that supports me and brings me back to normal, whatever that may be."

Giving Back: The Kelly Clark Foundation

Being a professional snowboarder doesn't come cheaply. The ski passes cost money, the gear costs money, and if you're going to operate at the level of Kelly Clark, a mountain school education costs big money. "Having something in place that allows you to focus on snowboarding and spend more time doing it is what you need to succeed at anything, and especially in snowboarding," said Kelly. The mountain school gave Kelly the broad base to become the snowboarding phenom she is today — but at a great cost. Sending a kid to a mountain school is nearly the equivalent of sending him or her to college — the expense is that great.

"I was frustrated with how expensive everything was, and I thought to myself, *If I'm frustrated with something, maybe I should do something about it instead of just being mad.* So I decided to start the Kelly Clark Foundation, which offers funding for kids who have needs and dreams to go to mountain schools and pursue their dreams in snowboarding."

Created in 2010, the Kelly Clark Foundation is a small foundation that helps pay tuition expenses at mountain schools for student-athletes ages 12 to 18 across the United States. Kelly's goal for the foundation is to give kids the opportunity to go after a dream that might not be possible otherwise. One of her favorite Scriptures is, "Hope deferred makes the heart sick, but a desire fulfilled is a tree of life" (Proverbs 13:12 ESV). It speaks to how she feels. God knows what is in our hearts, and he knows our desires and our passions. "It doesn't necessarily mean we're going to win or achieve all of our dreams, but I believe we're going to have a lot of life and fullness that comes in getting to do what's in our hearts."

For Kelly, it isn't just about people achieving their dreams or not; it's about getting the opportunity to try. The Kelly Clark Foundation looks for student-athletes who "honor integrity, generosity, fun, relationship, commitment, and excellence, believing that these values are vital for success in all areas of life." "Hopefully we'll be able to support more kids," said Kelly. "Some kids just never have that opportunity to even have potential."

Chapter 15

Let's Get Physical – Training to Be the Best

Snowboarding started out as a radical new extreme sport that gained legitimacy little by little. While it seems like all fun and games when riders are coming off rails and taking big air, there's more to it than just looking good while doing it. It takes skills, practice, determination, and training.

Kelly admitted when she was younger, she never really saw the importance of training and working out to maintain her body and her performance. Snowboarding was just cool—it was that alternative sport. "But being at the level of athletes that we are and competing, you'd be crazy to go to the Olympics as a downhill skier and not work out." Yet a number of riders haven't embraced the concept of serious physical training to be their best. "But the reality is, in snowboarding a lot of people do that," said Kelly.

87

She also admitted that snowboarding isn't always fun. "Sometimes I'm so sore that I don't even know why I'd want to go back up on the hill and practice that trick that I haven't been able to land." Kelly has a quote from Kris Vallotton (Kris & Kathy Vallotton Ministries) that she relates to: "Vision gives pain a purpose." Sometimes she has to step back to see where it is she wants to go and make decisions to help her get there. "So when things aren't fun, vision will help you keep going."

Vision, along with training, will hopefully get her where she wants to be. With a dozen years between her first Olympic appearance and what will be her fourth appearance in 2014, Kelly sees the value in training as she gets older. Not only does it help her prepare, but it also helps to prevent injuries. "I can take some really hard falls and not break my arm because I'm strong. My shoulder doesn't pop out because I've conditioned it and made it strong."

Additionally, Kelly sees that being fully committed to training led to two of the best seasons she's ever had, and she competed in more contests than ever before. "So there is fruit from it. I have a high value for training, and I know it is the key to success in my future. Training is a huge contributor to the length of my career."

How does Kelly get ready for her season? It starts with pre-season and off-season assessments. At the end of her season, Kelly goes through a series of tests. Her trainers look at things such as how much muscle mass she has; if one leg is bigger than the other one; or if she was injured, how it's affecting her. They check for flexibility in her shoulders, if her hips are tighter, how much lactic acid her body produces at different levels of endurance. "I mean, they test us every which way," said Kelly of the rigorous assessment. The trainers look for areas of weakness and write up programs accordingly.

Kelly and her fellow snowboarders are somewhat guinea pigs for how to develop training programs for snowboarders. It is one thing to have programs for football players, basketball players, and baseball players — athletes have been playing those sports for decades. But with the relative newness of the sport of snowboarding, the trainers are still developing what they consider to be the ideal body type for snowboarding and how to train for it.

Kelly's daily workouts look something like this: She takes one day off a week to let her body rest and recoup. Other than that, she has a mix of days that alternate between strength training, core training, agility exercises, and cardio workouts. She also does mobility exercises — addressing how the sport has the rider standing sideways all day with one leg stronger than the other, which can lead to imbalance in the body. "We really try to get our bodies symmetrical and flexible, mobility wise," said Kelly.

On most days Kelly performs at least two of the aforementioned activities. She works out two to three hours a day, and her workouts include a warmup, an activity, and a cool-down stretch. For example, Kelly may ride a bike four days a week, working toward maintaining her target heart rate to produce the endurance she needs to be competitive.

While it seems pretty intense, it's what Kelly needs to do to be prepared for the 2014 Winter Olympics. "I'll be thirty years old then. It's unheard of for someone to go to four Olympics from the United Sates, but that's my goal, that's my dream, and that's where I'm at now— I'm two years away—it's not unobtainable," said Kelly. "If I can maintain my body and keep it in shape and work on the strength, I don't hope to just make it—I hope to continue to be the best."

Chapter 16

The 2014 Winter Olympics – Sochi, Russia

Now that the 1080 is out there, Kelly has been working on new tricks to take with her to Russia. She's using her 2012–2013 season to solidify and perfect what she'll unleash on the world. "I know the placing that I want to get, I know what I'm going to be happy with, and I know what is obtainable for me, so I kind of mix all of those together. I throw them all into a big pot, and then I look to see if this is the run that is actually within reach and would potentially win the contest."

In a sport that is ever-changing and progressing, she hopes that the run she plans is the run that will be good enough to land her on the podium. It's a tricky situation for her to develop her run but not let too much info get out there, which would allow her competitors to come after her. She doesn't want to have them chase her down at the wrong time and beat her with the run that she thought no one else could do.

U.S. Snowboarding Halfpipe Coach Ricky Bower has worked with Kelly in the past, and he knows what it will take for her to win. He first met her at the U.S. Grand Prix in Maine back in 1998. He was a competitor at the time, but he noticed her because of how big she was going out of the pipe. What did he think? "This little girl rips."

Bower admires what Kelly did at age 18 during the 2002 Olympics. "She ushered in a new era for women by combining the technical aspects of flips and spins while going big doing it."

Going big is what Kelly does, and Bower saw her lay down probably one of the best runs of her career at the 2006 Olympics. The run included big tricks that would have put her in the top spot on the podium if she'd nailed her landing. However, the end result was a bad landing and fourth place. But the last two years have proven that Kelly doesn't give up or hold back.

"Now Kelly is in a league of her own," said Bower. "Her domination over the last two years has forced the other women to learn new tricks and do them bigger. Her biggest competition is her own teammates, and Kelly has been the wood that fuels the fire of progression on the U.S. Snowboarding team. She still goes bigger than anyone and can do 1080s with big Cab 7s after them. No one else in the world is even close to doing that. Her riding has raised the whole level of our team because as much as they all like Kelly, they really want to beat her."

Clark Family, used with permission of Mount Snow

Kelly on Mount Snow with her first "real" snowboard. She was eight years old.

And then there was the frontside 1080 at the 2011 Winter X Games. "Kelly has set the bar for women's snowboarding again," said Bower. This competitiveness might be the factor that allows the U.S. Women's Snowboarding team to dominate at the Olympics. "The U.S. Women are so good because they feed off of the progression of one another. They have an interesting relationship you don't find in most sports. They all seem to genuinely like each other. And in many cases, [they] are very good friends; while at the same time, they are [each other's] fiercest competition," said Bower. The tenacity they have for achieving a better performance, along with the number of halfpipes in the country, equals a formula for victory.

The one thing that separates Kelly from other snowboarders is that she's made it a priority to focus on the process rather than the outcome, according to Bower. This includes her learning new tricks and incorporating them into a run that she is pleased with. For some, competing throughout the season can lead to one letting the results dictate the training and outcome. This isn't the case with Kelly; she focuses on progressing rather than just doing enough to win, explained Bower.

Kelly's 16-win streak that ended in March 2012 proves Bower's point. Kelly works hard—not just at her tricks, but also in body conditioning and preparation. If her next season is anything like her last, she'll be grabbing big air, stomping out tricks, and riding the podium all the way to gold at the 2014 Olympics.

Snowboarding Tricks and Terms

Air—A jump or leap where the snowboard lifts off the ground.

Air-to-Fakie—A halfpipe trick where the wall is approached riding forward, no rotation is made in the air, and the boarder lands riding backward (or fakie).

Backcountry—Terrain outside of resort boundaries with no marked trails and natural obstacles like trees and cliffs.

Backside—A term originating from surfing, the direction in which you turn if you are traveling up a wave and turn so your back faces the wave. In snowboarding, it is used to describe your direction of rotation in which the rider spins clockwise in the air, if their left foot is facing down the hill (regular). It is the opposite of frontside.

Backside Air—Any aerial maneuver performed on the backside wall of the halfpipe.

Bail—A term used to describe crashing or falling; to escape out of a trick. (e.g., "He bailed and landed on his head.")

Bevel—The angle of a snowboard's steel edges. There are two bevels—the base bevel and the side edge bevel. The base bevel is the angle where the steel edge angles up from the flat base. The side bevel is the angle the steel edge is tilted from the sidewall. The greater the base bevel, the faster the board.

Boardercross—A competition where participants race through turns, banks, obstacles, and jumps in heats of four to five riders.

Boost—A term used to describe catching air off a jump. (e.g., "He boosted ten feet out of the halfpipe.")

Bonk—To intentionally hit (or bonk) a non-snow object, like a tree stump, with the snowboard. A bonk is a type of trick.

Bust—A term used the same as the verb "to do" only with emphasis. e.g., "He busted huge air over that tree."

Butter—Leaning on the nose of the board (like a nose manual) and swinging the tail of the board to the front.

Buttery—A term used to describe a snowboard with good flex.

Caballerial (Cab)—A halfpipe trick named after Steve Caballero (skateboard pro), which begins fakie, spins 360 degrees, and lands riding forward.

Chatter—When the snowboard vibrates unnecessarily. Usually this happens at higher speeds and through turns. Racers are always trying to reduce chatter in their boards so they can stay in control.

Corkskrew—An aerial fast and tight rotation in the halfpipe or off a jump.

Dampening—Reducing chatter (vibration) to increase handling and control. Structural modifications can be made to a snowboard or bindings to increase dampening.

Deck—The very top horizontal portion of the halfpipe wall where one can stand and look into the halfpipe. Photographers often shoot from this point. It is used as a walkway in order to hike to the top of the halfpipe.

Ding—A scratch or gouge in the base of the board. Dings can occur if a rider rides over a rock or hits a hard chunk of ice.

Duckfooted—A stance angle in which the toes are pointed outward like a duck's feet.

Edge—The smooth metal edges that run the perimeter of the snowboard.

Effective Edge—The length of steel edge on the snowboard that comes in contact with the snow when making turns. It is the effective part, which is used to make a turn. A longer effective edge makes for faster riding, while a shorter effective edge makes boards easier to turn and spin.

Eggflip—An eggplant where the rider flips over in order to re-enter the pipe instead of rotating 180 degrees.

Eggplant—A 180 backside rotated invert in which the front hand is planted on the lip of the halfpipe wall.

Faceplant—When a rider falls on his or her face.

Fakie—Riding backward or with your nondominant foot forward. Also referred to as "riding switch."

Flail—A term used to describe riding badly and out of control.

Flat Bottom—The flat area in a halfpipe that's between the two opposing transitional walls.

Forward Lean—The adjustable angle of degree to which the binding highbacks keep your ankles bent in a forward leaning position. Halfpipe riders increase their forward lean to gain speed. Park riders prefer a more relaxed forward lean, if any at all.

Frontside 1080—A trick involving three complete rotations and landing on the front edge of the board.

Freeriding—Snowboarding on all types of terrain (groomers, powder, backcountry) for fun with contests or competitions.

Freestyle Snowboarding—Mostly associated with riding the halfpipe, but which may also be used to describe jumps, spins, tricks, and riding on boxes or rails.

Fresh Fish Air—The backside version of the Stale Fish.

Front Hand—The hand closest to the nose of the snowboard.

Front Foot—The foot mounted closest to the nose of the board.

Frontside Air—An aerial maneuver performed on the toeside wall of a halfpipe.

Frontside Rotation—Rotating the direction your heel side is facing.

Goofy—Riding with the front foot forward or facing down the hill.

Grab—To grab either side of the snowboard in the air with the right or left hand.

Grommet (Grom)—Another name for a small, young snowboarder, especially one who is very "in to" snowboarding.

Halfpipe—A U-shaped snow structure built for freestyle snowboarding with opposing walls of the same height and pitch.

Handplant—A trick where one or both hands are planted on the lip of the halfpipe wall or obstacle and the rotation is either backside or frontside.

Highway—A large groove made by repeated riding in the same spot in the flat bottom and/or up the wall of a halfpipe.

Jam Session—A competition in which all riders perform in the halfpipe or park at the same time. One rider drops in after the next in no particular order.

Jib—Riding on something other than snow (e.g., rails, trees, garbage cans, logs).

Kicker—Large jump with a manmade or natural ramp.

Late—Putting an extra move in an aerial trick before landing.

Lip—The top edge of the halfpipe wall.

McTwist—Named after skateboarder Mike McGill, an inverted aerial where the athlete performs a 540-degree rotational flip. In other words, the rider approaches the halfpipe wall riding forward, becomes airborne, rotates 540 degrees in a backside direction while performing a front flip, and lands riding forward.

Nollie—Much like an Ollie, except the rider springs off of the nose instead of the tail.

Nose—The front end of the snowboard or tip.

Nose Bonk—To intentionally hit and rebound off of a natural or manmade object with the nose.

Nose Grab Air—During an aerial, the front hand grabs the nose of the snowboard.

Ollie—Borrowed from skateboarding, an Ollie is to get air by first lifting the front foot, springing off the back foot, and then landing on both feet.

Phat—Used to describe how exceptional something is.

Pipe Dragon—A grooming device used to groom halfpipes.

Poach—To ride closed terrain, like a roped-off trail, the park, or halfpipe.

Poser—One who pretends to be something one is not.

Pow—Snow.

Quarterpipe—A halfpipe with only one wall. It looks like a snow-sculpted shape, which contains a transition and a vertical, and is used as a jump to catch air.

Rail—(1.) A snowboard obstacle resembling a handrail for stairs; (2.) The sidewall and an edge of a snowboard.

Railing—A term used to describe making fast and hard turns.

Rear Hand—The hand closest to the tail of the snowboard.

Rear Foot—The foot mounted closest to the tail.

Regular Footed—Riding on a snowboard with the left foot facing downhill or closest to the nose.

Rodeo Flip—An inverted frontside 540 off of a straight jump. In the halfpipe, it is more like performing a 540-degree rotation, which is inverted and off-axis.

Run—A slope or trail.

Running Length—The length of the base of the snowboard, which touches the snow.

Shifty Air—When the upper torso and lower body are twisted in opposite directions and then returned to normal. Usually the front leg is boned and no grab is involved.

Sketching—The act of riding along precariously and nearly falling.

Sideslip—Sliding sideways down a slope. Beginners often sideslip when they are learning.

Slopestyle—A freestyle event in which the competitor rides over a series of various kinds of jumps, boxes, and rails. He or she is then judged on the performance of tricks and maneuvers.

Soft Boots—Snowboard boots designed for use in freestyle and freeride snowboarding. Boots are soft and pliable and allow a large range of motion while maintaining sufficient support.

Snurfer—The original snowboard made in 1965 by Sherman Popper. It did not have bindings or edges, but it had a rope attached to the nose for steering.

Spin—To turn in the air.

Stoked—An alternate term for the word *psyched*. In other words, to be excited.

Stomp—A term used to describe a good landing made by a rider.

Switchstance (Switch)—Riding with your non-dominant foot forward. Also referred to as "riding fakie."

Tail—The rear tip of the snowboard.

Tail Bonk—To intentionally hit and bounce off an object, either natural or manmade, with the tail of the snowboard.

Tail Grab Air—The rear hand grabs the tail of the snowboard.

Toe Edge—The edge of the snowboard closest to the toes; the opposite of the heel edge.

Toe Overhang/Drag—When the toe hangs off the edge of the board and potentially drags in the snow. Toe drags occur if the binding is set up incorrectly or if the board is too small for the rider.

Transition (Tranny)—The radial curved section of a halfpipe wall between the flat bottom and the vertical.

Traverse—To ride perpendicular or diagonal to the fall line.

Vertical (Vert)—The vertical top portion of a wall in a halfpipe, which allows the snowboarder to boost into the air.

Wack—Something that is not good.

Wall—The transition and vertical section of a halfpipe.

Sources

Bane, Collin, "White, Hight win U.S. Open Halfpipe," March 10, 2012, ESPN.com, http://espn.go.com/action/snowboarding/story/_/id/7664326/thirtieth-annual-burton-us-open-halfpipe-wraps-stratton-vt, accessed March 11, 2012.

Branch, John, "Torah Bright Wins Women's Halfpipe," February 18, 2010, NY Times.com, www.nytimes.com/2010/02/19/sport/olympics/, accessed May 7, 2012.

Brown, Gerry and Charistine Frantz, "Winter Olympics: Snowboarding," Infoplease, http://www.infoplease.com/spot/winter-olympics-snowboarding.html, accessed July 5, 2011.

Brown, Shaun and Barbara, Cornick, "Kelly Clark: Head Over Heels in Love, CBN.com, http://www.cbn.com/entertainment/Sports/700club_kellyclark021006.aspx, accessed November 14, 2011.

"Burke in Critical Condition After Fall," January 12, 2012, ESPN. com. http://espn.go.com/action/freeskiing/story/_/id/7447871/freeskier-sarah-burke-seriously-injured-utah-halfpipe-fall, accessed May 2, 2012.

Cazeneuve, Brian, "Ageless Snowboarder Kelly Clark Wins Gold Again at X Games," February 2, 2011, Inside Olympic Sports, SI.com, http://sportsillustrated.cnn.com/2011/writers/brian_cazeneuve/02/02/olympic.notebook/index.html, accessed July 5, 2011.

Clark, Kelly, "Kelly Clark – I've Never Been More Free," Beyond the Ultimate, http://www.beyondtheultimate.org/athletes/Kelly-Clark.aspx, accessed November 14, 2011.

"Clark's Big Final Run Proves To Be a Golden One," February 11, 2001, ESPN, http://sports.espn.go.com/oly/winter02/snowboard/news?id=1326727, accessed August 15, 2012.

Crane, Lee, "History of Snowboarding Part 1—1960s—1970s," TransWorldSnowboarding.com, http://ussnowboarding.com/snowboarding/history-snowboarding-part-i-1960s-1970s, accessed January 27, 2012.

Crane, Lee, "History of Snowboarding Part 2—1980s," TransWorldSnowboarding.com, http://ussnowboarding.com/snowboarding/history-snowboarding-part-2-1980s, accessed January 27, 2012.

Crane, Lee, "History of Snowboarding Part 3—1990s," TransWorldSnowboarding.com, http://ussnowboarding.com/snowboarding/history-snowboarding-part-3-1990s, accessed January 27, 2012.

Dupont, Kevin Paul, "Bright, Shiny Night for Australia," February 19, 2010, Boston.com, http://www.boston.com/sports/other_sports/olympics/articles/2010/02/19/bright_shiny_night_for_australia/, accessed August 15, 2012.

"Developmental Reading Disorder," December 10, 2010, U.S. National Library of Medicine, www.ncbi.nlm.nih.gov/pubmedhealth/pmH0002379/, accessed August 16, 2012.

Ellsworth, Tim, "Olympics: Faith Made Kelly Clark's Snowboarding 'A Lot More Free'," February 17, 2010, Baptist Press, http://www.bpnews.net/bpnews.asp?id=32312, accessed December 19, 2011.

"From Competitive Snurfer to Vancouver—The History of Snowboarding," May 17, 2009, Random History and Word Origins for the Curious Mind, http://www.randomhistory.com/history-of-snowboarding.html, accessed April 24, 2012.

Herrie, Angela, "How Does A Grease Trap Work?" eHow.com, www.ehow.com/how-does_4886521_grease-trap-work.html, accessed August 15, 2012.

"History of Olympic Snowboarding, ABC-of-Snowboarding, http://www.abc-of-snowboarding.com/info/olympic-snowboarding-history.asp, accessed April 24, 2012.

"History of Snowboarding—The Birth of the Snowboard & Boarding Vacations," Vermont Living Magazine, http://www.vtliving.com/snowboard/history.shtml, accessed April 24, 2012.

"History of Snowboarding," BulgariaSki.com, http://www.bulgariaski.com/snowboarding.shtml, accessed April 24, 2012.

"History of Snowboarding," Oracle Think Quest, http://library.thinkquest.org/3885/history.html, accessed April 24, 2012.

"How to Apply," The Kelly Clark Foundation.org, http://www.kellyclarkfoundation.org/, accessed August 16, 2012.

"How To Share Your Faith Using Kelly Clark," Dare 2 Share Youth Ministry Resources, https://www.dare2share.org/culturecommission/kelly-clark, accessed July 5, 2011.

"How To: Snowboarding Terms," The House Outdoor Gear, www.the-house.com/portal/snowboarding-terms/, accessed July 16, 2012.

Judd, Ron, "Snowboarding – Winter Olympics Spectator's Guide," December 21, 2009, The Seattle Times, http://seattletimes.nwsource.com/html/olympics/2010501784_snowboarding.html, accessed May 4, 2012.

"Kelly Clark." Burton.com, http://www.burton.com/on/demandware.store/Sites-Burton_US-Site/default/Team-Rider?rid=kelly-clark, accessed July 16, 2012.

"Kelly Clark," US Snowboarding, http://ussnowboarding.com/athletes/kelly-clark, accessed April 29, 2012.

"Kelly Clark," Ride With Us, US Snowboarding, http://www.ussnowboarding.com/athletes/athlete?athleteID=1209, accessed November 14, 2011.

Lazzari, Zach, "Olympic Snowboarding Half Pipe Rules," Trails.com, http://www.trails.com/facts_13442_olympic-half-pipe-snowboarding-rules.html, accessed May 4, 2012.

Lewis, Mike, "Snowboarding Slopestyle Added to 2014 Olympics," July 5, 2011, Transworld Business, http://business.transworld.net/67266/features/snowboarding-slopestyle-added-to-2014-olympics/, accessed July 5, 2011.

MacAuthur, Paul, "The Top Ten Important Moments in Snowboarding History," February 5, 2010, Smithsonian.com, http://www.smithsonianmag.com/history-archaeology/The-Top-Ten-Most-Important-Moments-in-Snowboarding-History.html, accessed April 24, 2012.

Michaelis, Vicki, "'02 Halfpipe Winner Kelly Clark Keeps Feet on Ground," February 10, 2010, USA Today, http://www.usatoday.com/sports/olympics/vancouver/snowboarding/2010-02-04-clark-halfpipe_N.htm, accessed May 4, 2012.

Murphy, Austin, "Stoked Italiana," February 20, 2006, SI Vault, http://sportsillustrated.cnn.com/vault/article/magazine/MAG1105882/index.htm, accessed May 4, 2012.

"The Modern Olympic Games," The Olympic Museum, http://www.olympic.org/Documents/Reports/EN/en_report_668.pdf, accessed August 16, 2012.

"Olympic Games." sochi.ru 2014. http://www.sochi2014.com/en/games/sport/olympic-games/sports/skiing/snowboard/, accessed August 16, 2012.

O'Neil, Devon, "Kelly Clark Wins Fourth SuperPipe Gold," January 27, 2012, ESPN.com, http://espn.go.com/action/xgames/winter/2012/story/_/id/7499201/kelly-clark-wins-winter-x-2012-women-snowboard-superpipe, accessed May, 2, 2012.

O'Neil, Devon and Collin Bane, "It Happened at Winter X, January 30, 2012, ESPN.com, http://espn.go.com/action/xgames/winter/2012/story/_/id/7518434/top-stories-winter-x-games-aspen-2012, accessed May 2, 2012.

Pells, Eddie, "Hannah Teter Wins Silver, Kelly Clark Takes Bronze in Women's Halfpipe," February 18, 2010, Huff Post Sports, The Huffington Post, http://www.huffingtonpost.com/2010/02/18/hannah-teter-wins-silver-_n_468342.html, accessed May 7, 2012.

Pelletier, Jared, "Snowboarding History," Snowboarding History.com, www.snowboardinghistory.com, accessed August 15, 2012.

Sources

Pierce, Vanessa, "Kelly Clark's Success Funds Future Stars' Training," November 29, 2011, ESPN W.com, http://espn.go.com/espnw/journeys-victories/7294297/kelly-clark-success-funds-future-stars-training, accessed January 13, 2012.

"Pipe Dream," Posted February 10, 2002, CNN Sports Illustrated.com, http://sportsillustrated.cnn.com/olympics/2002/snowboarding/news/2002/02/10/womens_halfpipe_ap/, accessed August 16, 2012.

"Sarah Burke Dies From Injuries," January 15, 2012, ESPN Action Sports, ESPN.com, http://espn.go.com/action/freeskiing/story/_/id/7466421/sarah-burke-dies-injuries-suffered-utah, accessed May 2, 2012.

Schultz, Tawya, "The History of Winter X Games Part 1," SnowBoard magazine, http://snowboardmag.com/stories/history-winter-x-games-part–1, accessed August 15, 2012.

Schwartz, Shannon, "The History of Snowboarding – From Garages to the Olympics," September 10, 2009, TheHistoryOf.net, http://www.thehistoryof.net/history-of-snowboarding.html, accessed April 24, 2012

"Sims Did It First," Simsnow.com, http://www.simsnow.com/news/category/tom-sims#/history/firsts, accessed April 24, 2012.

Sine, Lindsey, "Mammoth Snowboarders Do Well in Halfpipe on Home Terrain," March 5, 2011, Lake Tahoe News, http://www.laketahoenews.net/2011/03/mammoth-snowboarders-do-well-in-halfpipe-on-home-terrain/, accessed August 17, 2012.

"Skiing—Snowboard: Participation During the History of the Olympic Winter Games," November, 2011, International Olympic Committee, http://www.olympic.org/Assets/OSC%20Section/pdf/QR_sports_winter/Sports_Olympiques_ski_snowboard_eng.pdf, accessed August, 17, 2012.

"Snowboard Equipment and History," Olympic.org, http://www.olympic.org/snowboard-equipment-and-history?tab=history, accessed May 4, 2012.

"Snowboarding Glossary," Adventure Sports Online, www.adventuresportsonline.com/snowboardglossary.htm#Line, accessed July 17, 2012.

"Snowboarding History—Origin of Snowboard," ABC-of-Snowboarding, http://www.abc-of-snowboarding.com/snowboardinghistory.asp, accessed April 24, 2012.

"Snowboarding Terms," www.snowboarding2.com/misc/terms/index.php, accessed July 17, 2012.

"Snowboarding Tricks—Steezy Snowboard Tricks," January 19, 2012, How to 360 Snowboard, http://www.howto360snowboard.com/snowboarding-tricks-steezy-snowboard-tricks/, accessed March 12, 2012.

Symms, John, "Freeski Community Rallies Behind Burke, January 13, 2012, ESPN.com, http://espn.go.com/action/freeskiing/story/_/id/7460497/freeski-community-rallies-injured-sarah-burke, accessed May 2, 2012.

"Tributes to Burke Begin Before X Games," January 25, 2012, SI.com, http://sportsillustrated.cnn.com/vault/article/web/COM1194201/index.htm, accessed April 29, 2012.

"US Open Snowboarding Championship History Highlights," Burton US Open, http://opensnowboarding.com/History.aspx?openid=USO, accessed April 24, 2012.

"Vancouver's Dream Team," February 2012, The Oprah Magazine, Oprah.com, http://www.oprah.com/entertainment/The-Friendship-Between-the-US-Winter-Olympics-Female-Snowboarders, accessed March 12, 2012.

Voje, Julian, "The Beginning of Snowboarding," May 22, 2005, The History of Snowboarding, http://www.sbhistory.de/ussnowboarding.com, accessed April 24, 2012.

Wang, Cynthia, "Third Time the Charm for Kelly Clark on the Olympic Halfpipe?" February 18, 2010, People, http://www.people.com/people/article/0,,20345285,00.html, accessed August 17, 2012.

Yen, Yi-Wyn, "A Higher Power," February 14, 2006, SI.com, http://sportsillustrated.cnn.com/2006/olympics/2006/writers/02/13/clark.pipe/, accessed April 29, 2012.

Speed to Glory:
The Cullen Jones Story

Natalie Davis Miller

He conquered the thing that nearly took his life. At five years old, Cullen Jones nearly drowned. While some people might stay away from water after that, Jones conquered his fear when his mother enrolled him in a swimming class. Not only did he learn to swim, he quickly found that he was a good swimmer ... and would become one of the world's best. Discover how faith, courage, and hard work led Jones to win an Olympic gold medal and set a new world record in his event. Find out what can happen when you overcome fear and strive to become all God calls you to be. Includes a personal note from Cullen Jones.

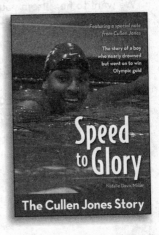

Available in stores and online!

We want to hear from you. Please send your comments about this book to us in care of zreview@zondervan.com. Thank you.